# The Proper Care of
# PARROTS

**TW-101**

**Title page:** Orange-fronted Conures, Canary-winged Parakeets, and a Tui Parakeet.


**Photographs and illustrations:** David Alderton, Glen S. Axelrod, Dr. Herbert R. Axelrod, Cliff Bickford, Horst Bielfeld, Courtesy of Bird Depot, Dr. E. W. Burr, Tom Caravaglia, Chellman & Petrulla, John Daniel, Michael DeFreitas, Isabelle Francais, Michael Gilroy, Earl Grossman, Ray Hanson, Fred Harris, Dieter Hoppe, Ralph Kaehler, Harry V. Lacey, P. Leysen, Don Mathews, Diane McCarty, Susan C. Miller, Max Mills, A. J. Mobbs, Dr. E. J. Mulawka, Eric Peake, John R. Quinn, Courtesy of Midori Shibo, Robert Pearcy, Elaine Radford, Nancy Richmond, Mervin F. Roberts, L. Robinson, Routedale, Vince Serbin, Carol Thiem, Tony Tilford, Louise Van der Meid, Courtesy of Vogelpark Walsrode, Dr. M. M. Vriends, Wayne Wallace, R. Williams.

Distributed in the UNITED STATES by T.F.H. Publications, Inc., One T.F.H. Plaza, Neptune City, NJ 07753; in CANADA to the Pet Trade by H & L Pet Supplies Inc., 27 Kingston Crescent, Kitchener, Ontario N2B 2T6; Rolf C. Hagen Ltd., 3225 Sartelon Street, Montreal 382 Quebec; in CANADA to the Book Trade by Macmillan of Canada (A Division of Canada Publishing Corporation), 164 Commander Boulevard, Agincourt, Ontario M1S 3C7; in ENGLAND by T.F.H. Publications, PO Box 15, Waterlooville PO7 6BQ; in AUSTRALIA AND THE SOUTH PACIFIC by T.F.H. (Australia) Pty. Ltd., Box 149, Brookvale 2100 N.S.W., Australia; in NEW ZEALAND by Ross Haines & Son, Ltd., 82 D Elizabeth Knox Place, Panmure, Auckland, New Zealand; in the PHILIPPINES by Bio-Research, 5 Lippay Street, San Lorenzo Village, Makati, Rizal; in SOUTH AFRICA by Multipet Pty. Ltd., P.O. Box 35347, Northway, 4065, South Africa. Published by T.F.H. Publications, Inc. Manufactured in the United States of America by T.F.H. Publications, Inc.

# The Proper Care of
# PARROTS

**Martin Skinner**

# CONTENTS

One of the features of the group of birds known as parrots is the brilliance of coloration that characterizes so many of the species, whether large or small. For may people, the large, spectacular macaws typify the parrots; at the other extreme but equally colorful are the little fig parrots shown here.

# *Introducing Parrots*

There are over 300 different species in the parrot family, many of which are popular as pets and aviary occupants. They range in size from the large macaws, which may exceed 40 in. (100 cm) in length, down to the tiny pigmy parrots found on New Guinea and neighboring islands, which are only a tenth of this size.

This book will help you to choose the type of parrot which appeals to you, by explaining the requirements of the different groups. Some are more suitable as pets than others. Most will also nest in aviary surroundings, although breeding successes are easier to obtain in certain cases, depending on the species concerned. Here you will find wide coverage of all the main short-tailed parrots, as well as many others such as the macaws, lories and lorikeets.

## WHAT ARE PARROTS?

Parrots can be easily recognized by their beaks. They all have a distinctly curved upper bill, which fits over the protruding lower part of the beak. They also have a fairly distinctive perching grip, with two toes of each foot directly forward over the perch, and the other two gripping behind.

Parrots often use their feet like hands, for holding food. Studies have shown that, in a way similar to left and right-handed people, so parrots show individual preferences for using one foot or the other, when feeding in this way. The majority of parrots are also very colorful birds, with green, red, yellow, and blue coloration featuring strongly in their plumage.

Fossil ancestors of today's parrots date back at least 30 million years, with the earliest remains from France, suggesting that these birds used to have a much wider distribution in the past. Parrots are now confined largely, but not exclusively, to tropical areas. They can sometimes be seen in Texas, for example, and range southward from here to southern areas of South America.

Little is known about the evolution of parrots. Their nearest surviving relatives are considered

Superb Parrot, *Polytelis swainsonii*, male.

**Facing page:** Scarlet (*Ara macao*) and Blue-and-Gold (*Ara ararauna*) macaws.

Parrots have successfully captured the imagination of people the world over. Here macaws native to the Americas have been rendered in an Oriental tradition of painting.

by some people to be the cuckoos, and touracos from Africa. But analysis of egg-white (albumen) proteins suggest a closer affiliation with pigeons.

## THE POPULARITY OF PARROTS

Parrots have been kept since the dawn of history, with references to talking birds being found in early classical references dating back centuries. In the Middle Ages, parrots were highly-prized gifts for royalty. Frederick II (1194-1250) had a favorite Umbrella Cockatoo which was presented to him by the Sultan of Babylon. Columbus, following his epic voyage to the New World in 1492, brought back a pair of Cuban Amazon Parrots *(Amazona leucocephala)* for his

In recent years, the smaller macaws, such as the Red-shouldered (*Ara nobilis*), have received increasing avicultural attention.

Yellow-naped Macaws, *Ara auricollis.*

Charles II (1661-1685) was such a favorite that on its demise, it was stuffed and is now the oldest surviving example of avian taxidermy.

Parrots normally have a lifespan measured in decades, which is far longer than that of most other household pets. Perhaps not surprisingly, the larger species, such as the Blue-fronted Amazon, may often live for over 50 years. The purchase of a parrot can therefore become a lifelong commitment.

Their attractive

patron, Queen Isabella of Spain.

During the next century, King Henry VIII of England (1509-1547) was the proud owner of a Grey Parrot, which is known to have been a talented mimic. Another, belonging to a mistress of

**Facing page:** The three parrots shown here can all be expected to live long lives as companion animals: Blue-fronted Amazon (*Amazona aestiva*), Moluccan Cockatoo (*Cacatua moluccensis*), and Blue-and-Gold Macaw (*Ara ararauna*).

appearance, coupled with their natural tameness and curiosity are some of the reasons for the popularity of parrots. Whether keeping a pet, or a larger collection of parrots in aviary surroundings, you will be assured of hours of

Sun Conures, *Aratinga solstitialis.*

fascination with these birds.

## OBTAINING PARROTS

Your local pet store may well be able to help you. Even if they don't have a particular species in stock, they could be prepared to obtain parrots for you. Some stores tend to specialize in birds, and obviously, it is best to contact one of these in your neighborhood. You may be able to find them by looking in the telephone book.

Alternatively, seek out one of the specialist bird-keeping magazines from a newsstand, as such stores often advertise here. They will have stock purchased from breeders, and also from specialized imports.

International trade in parrots is tightly

The Malabar Parakeet, *Psittacula columboides*, is one of the less familiar species among the ring-necked parakeets.

The Grey-cheeked, or Orange-flanked, Parakeet, *Brotogeris pyrrhopterus*.

Disease (Fowl Pest). This can have devastating effects on chickens, and other birds. The virus itself can be spread easily through the air, from one poultry unit to another, rapidly creating a major epidemic.

regulated, both for conservation and health reasons. Permits must be obtained in advance from the relevant authorities for the importation of parrots. The main fear which has led to the establishment of quarantine procedures is the possibility that imported parrots could be infected with Newcastle

## CHOOSING PARROTS

If you want a pet parrot, then it is vital to choose a young bird, preferably one that is hand-raised and has no fear of people. There are various means of recognizing immature birds as distinct from adult parrots. These are listed in conjunction with the various species covered later in the book. Even for breeding purposes, it may be worthwhile acquiring young stock. You can then be certain of the age of the birds, whereas once they have molted into adult plumage, it will be virtually impossible to judge their age unless, of course, they are banded with a closed ring. This should reveal the year that the parrots hatched, and also the breeder's initials. Since bands of this type can be fitted only when the chicks are about a week or so old, they provide a reliable indication of the parrot's age.

Currently, legislation increasingly requires evidence of captive breeding of parrots, such as is provided by closed banding of nestlings. The chick shown here belongs to the best known parrot species, the Budgerigar.

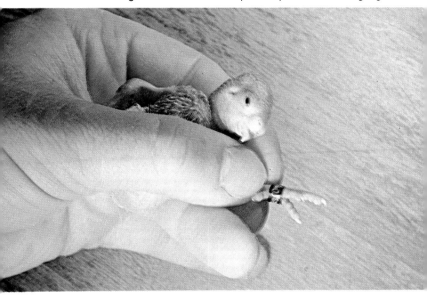

Healthy parrots appear bright-eyed and alert, although if they are imported, their feathering may be rather scruffy. This need not be a cause for concern, except in the case of cockatoos, which are susceptible to the viral disease often known as 'Feather Rot', for which there is presently no cure. Affected birds have stunted plumage, which often appears slightly brownish in color, contrasting with their normal white plumage. It is a progressive disease and ultimately proves fatal.

If the feathering appears normal however, apart from a bald patch on the chest, this is more likely to be a sign of feather-plucking. This problem afflicts not only cockatoos, but also other parrots, especially Greys and macaws. Feather-plucking is most commonly seen in pet parrots housed on their own, and can be a difficult problem to overcome successfully.

Always look at a prospective purchase

The Maroon-bellied Conure, *Pyrrhura frontalis.*

Feather plucking restricted to the breast area, as seen in this Blue-and-Gold Macaw, probably arose from a complex of inadequacies in management, and it will likely prove difficult to arrest.

quietly for a few moments from a distance, rather than standing directly next to the parrot. If the bird appears to be wheezing, or if its

**Above:** The Turquoisine Parakeet, *Neophema pulchella.*

**Facing page:** Tidy feathering and bright-eyed alertness are signs of well-being even in wild-caught parrots. Shown here is the Mexican Parrotlet, (*Forpus cyanopygius*), one of the smallest parrots, only a few inches in length.

is quite normal for a parrot to have only one foot on the perch, but it should then move readily when its cage is approached.

Check the food pots. There should be evidence, especially with a young parrot, that it is eating properly on its own. Seed husks will normally be present on the floor of the cage. The parrot's droppings should be well-formed, and never very watery. Also, check the feathering surrounding the vent region, between the legs. This should appear clean and free from any sign of fecal contamination.

Closer examination will reveal if the parrot is showing signs of weight loss. This is evident by muscle wasting over the

plumage is fluffed up, it is likely to prove a source of concern, and is best avoided. When resting, it

**Above:** Bronze-winged Parrot, *Pionus chalcopterus.*

Ask the vendor to hold the parrot so that you can run your fingers down the breastbone to check this health indicator.

## CATCHING AND HANDLING PARROTS

The method used will depend to some extent on the size of the bird, and its enclosure. Parrots in cages should be caught by hand, while cloth nets with well-padded rims are useful in aviaries, for all but the very largest species. These can usually be obtained from pet stores.

Smooth gloves should always be worn to protect against bites, because even the smaller species can give a nasty nip, and are quite capable of drawing blood. Woolen or knitted gloves of any kind are unsuitable, as the

breastbone, which runs along the underside of the body, in the mid-line. A bird which is not eating properly, or has been sick for a period of time, will have distinct hollows on either side of the bone.

The formidable-looking beak of the Slender-billed Conure, *Enicognathus leptorhynchus,* represents an adaptation for extracting seeds from araucaria trees.

**Above:** Red-rumped Parrots, *Psephotus haematonotus*, a pair.

**Facing page:** The Monk, or Quaker, Parakeet has shown itself well suited to aviculture. However, its potential to become an agricultural pest has caused its sale to be prohibited in some areas.

Thicker gardening gloves are to be recommended for handling macaws, cockatoos and other large parrots. It is also advisable to wear two pairs of gloves, with a thinner inner pair underneath, so that should the parrot bite the glove, the impact on the finger beneath will be minimal.

The major drawback to wearing gloves when handling parrots is that the natural sensitivity of the fingers is much reduced. Extra care should be taken to ensure that the parrot is restrained effectively, but gently. Handling a parrot is relatively straightforward, and you will soon gain in confidence, even if you

birds will get their feet entangled in this type of material, and they offer little protection against the bird's beak.

have never handled any bird before. Once aviary parrots are established in their surroundings, you will not need to catch them regularly in any event.

As a guide for a right-handed person, hold the bird's head between the first and second fingers of the left hand. With the wings restrained by the palm of the hand, the rest of the body can be secured using the thumb on the parrot's right side, and the other fingers on

**Facing page:** The Cape Parrot, *Poicephalus robustus*, is characterized by a formidable beak.

**Below:** Padded gloves are used to restrain a Nanday Conure, *Nandayus nenday*, for claw trimming.

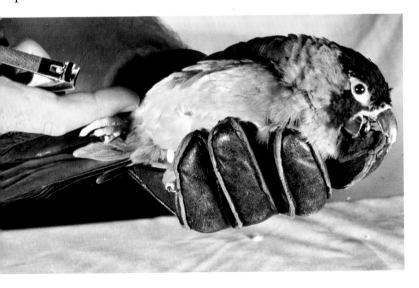

the left. If you're left-handed, simply use your right hand for holding the parrot instead, reversing the procedure.

The majority of parrots will not struggle when restrained in this way, but for the large macaws, you may need to use both hands for the purpose.

You can then examine the parrot quite easily, running a finger over its breastbone for example, and are also well-protected from being bitten. Never press on the parrot's neck however, at any stage, since this is likely to interfere with its breathing.

**Below:** Trimming wing feathers to inhibit flight, as with this Cockatiel, is one of the most common occasions that call for handling the bird.

**Facing page:** Even small parrots like the Cockatiel have enough strength in their bills to cause a painful bite.

**Above:** The feathers important to flight, seen here in the Turquoisine Parakeet, *Neophema pulchella*, often contain dark pigments which serve to strengthen them.

**Facing page:** Controlling a bird is best accomplished with its head between the index and middle fingers, as with this Budgerigar. The kind of restraint required will vary, of course, according to the bird's size and tameness and what needs to be accomplished.

## MOVING PARROTS

Having decided on a purchase, you will need a secure container to carry the bird home. Although cardboard boxes are sometimes used, these are unsuitable even for the smallest species. You will need to include ventilation holes, and the parrot is likely to start gnawing at these, or any other site of weakness, such as the floor, and it will then escape.

It's much better to use a proper carrying box, of the type sold for cats. Ask at your pet store. One of the covered types of carriers is to be preferred, rather than an all-mesh design. Line the floor with

**Facing page:** The design of this cardboard shipping container ensures ventilation even if it is placed close to other cartons. Different sizes are available to accommodate various birds appropriately, such as the Grey Parrot shown here.

**Below:** Transport cages of this type are handy for short trips and to hold birds while changing cages, and so forth.

### ... BIRDS ..

### .. CATS ...

### ... ANIMALS ...

### ... DOGS ..

.. FISH ...

cats, birds, fish, small animals, etc.), plus books dealing with more purely scientific aspects of the animal world (such as books about fossils, corals, sea shells, whales and octopuses). Whether you are a beginner or an advanced hobbyist you will find exactly what you're looking for among our complete listing of books. For a free catalog fill out the form on the other side of this page and mail it today. All T.F.H. books are recyclable.

Since 1982, *Tropical Fish Hobbyist* has been the source of accurate, up-to-the-minute, and fascinating information on every facet of the aquarium hobby. Join the more than 50,000 devoted readers worldwide who wouldn't miss a single issue.

newspaper first, so the parrot will have a firm base on which to rest.

Carriers are better than cages, as the parrots can travel largely in the dark. Also, you may get bitten through the bars as you maneuver a cage in and out of a car, whereas there should be no risk of this using a proper carrier.

It is useful to know what the parrots are being fed, especially with a young hand-raised bird. Nectar-feeders are also sensitive to sudden changes in diet, so try to follow their existing diet closely for the first week or so, until they have settled in with you. Changes can then be carried out gradually over a period of time, allowing the parrots to readjust to their new food. This lessens the likelihood of digestive problems arising.

If you have other parrots, be sure to keep new arrivals separate from established stock for at least a fortnight. This gives the new birds an opportunity to settle down, and is a useful precaution on health grounds as well.

Remember that recently-imported parrots acquired during the late summer or winter will need to be housed indoors in temperate climates until spring. They should be transferred to an outside aviary only when the weather is dry, and unlikely to turn cold again.

In any event, keep the parrots confined in the shelter part of their enclosure at first, so they will soon discover their food and water containers here. Then, when you do let them out into the flight, they should readily return inside.

Keep a close watch on the parrots at this stage, and check that they are in fact eating properly. If you first allow them to venture out into the flight in the morning, they should have returned to the shelter to feed at some stage during the day, before darkness falls. Any parrot which appears fluffed up may not actually be sick, but simply might not have

A Goffin's Cockatoo (*Cacatua goffini*) in a pet carrier. Also used for other animals, carriers suit parrots very well. For longer trips, a dish of dry food can be included. In place of water, which could be lost through spillage, the chopped fruit will satisfy a bird's thirst.

eaten. Under these circumstances, move the bird back into the shelter for a few more days.

If you have a parrot whose wing feathers have been clipped, remember that this will restrict its flight. Since many parrots

**Facing page:** Imported parrots, such as these Red-masked Conures (*Aratinga erythrogenys*) often carry plain wire bands.

**Below:** Dishes that attach to the cage wire allow food intake to be monitored easily, as with these Lutino Cockatiels.

enjoy climbing around their aviary, rather than flying, this is often not a noticeable handicap. Only if the bird is suddenly frightened will it become a problem, as then it may well attempt to fly, and end up on the ground.

Therefore, take care to move around cautiously when you are in the aviary so as to not cause a disturbance. In time, the cut feathers will be molted, and replaced by a new set, then enabling the parrot to fly without any difficulty. Parrots molt annually, so in fact it should not be long before these clipped flight feathers are being shed.

Split bands bearing numbers are useful to identify parrots, such as Budgerigars, that are bred in quantity.

Cockatoo with clipped primary feathers. Limiting flying ability is helpful in settling and taming nervous birds.

Parrots of widely different sizes, such as a Masked Lovebird and a Moluccan Cockatoo, should not be housed together.

# *Housing Parrots*

Whether you are keeping one parrot, or several, you will need to have suitable accommodation, in the form of cages available. The size and type of cage required is influenced to a great extent by the species concerned. For example, parrotlets can be kept quite satisfactorily in budgerigar-type cages, but they would escape easily through the mesh of many larger parrot cages.

If you are in doubt as to which type of cage is most suitable, ask your pet store for advice. Here you should find a good range of cages on offer, and other designs may be available to order. For

**Above:** A good rule of thumb to assess cage size: it should allow the parrot (here a Yellow-naped Amazon, *Amazona auropalliata*) to extend its wings fully.

**Facing page:** Cages of wrought iron provide durable housing for the largest parrots, such as the Blue-and-Gold Macaw, *Ara ararauna*.

smaller parrots, cages with detachable plastic bases are easy to clean thoroughly, but any plastic accessible to the birds will probably be gnawed over a period of time.

The trend in housing larger species, such as cockatoos and macaws, is to opt for cage panels, rather than a fairly small cage. These can then be clipped together to create a much

bigger unit, at relatively low cost. They are also favored by pet stores, because the panels can be stored flat, taking up less space than traditional cages.

Some cage panels are equipped with separate bases, whereas in other cases, you will need to use the mesh panels to form this part of the cage as well. It may also be possible to fit casters, enabling you to wheel the unit around the home. This can be especially useful for cleaning purposes.

Check that the entry door in cages of this type gives you easy access to the interior, so you can feed the parrots and clean out the floor easily.

Perches should be fixed firmly in place, with one near the food pot. You must be sure that these are not so close to the ends of the cage that the parrot is constantly rubbing its tail here, as it perches.

**Above:** Transport cages can also be used to hold a parrot while the cage is being cleaned or repaired.

**Facing page:** A cage cover can be employed if the parrot cage is situated in location where lights are kept on late.

It will be worth adding a padlock around the door-opening of cages for the larger parrots. Otherwise, there is a risk that they may soon learn

to undo the catch here, and escape into the room, often when you are out. This is obviously not to be recommended. If you use a combination lock for this purpose, there will be

The typical parrot cage has a removable tray to facilitate cleaning out droppings and seed hulls.

no need to worry about keys when you do open the cage door.

Aviary panels are constructed of welded wire having a mesh size suited to the parrot species that will be accommodated. This Budgerigar is enclosed with three-eighths-inch mesh.

## AVIARIES

As with cages, the design of the aviary will be influenced to some

One of the numerous subspecies of the Brown-throated Conure, *Aratinga pertinax*.

**Above:** Perches in a cage should be located so that droppings are directed away from food items and drinking water.

**Facing page:** If a cage will have two occupants, such as the Budgerigar and Cockatiel housed here, both birds should be introduced to their new home at the same time, so that neither will feel territorial priority.

extent by the parrots which you decide to keep. Generally, smaller species are less demanding in terms of their housing needs, and thus cheaper to accommodate as a result. Aviaries are usually comprised of two parts. There is a wire mesh flight, and an

## TABLE OF FLIGHT SIZES

| SPECIES | LENGTH | | BREADTH | | HEIGHT | |
|---|---|---|---|---|---|---|
| | Feet | Meters | Feet | Meters | Feet | Meters |
| Lovebirds, etc. | 9 | 2.7 | 3 | 0.9 | 6 | 1.8 |
| Other Aftican Parrots | 10 | 3.0 | 4 | 1.2 | 6 | 1.8 |
| Lories, Amazons, *Pionus* | 12 | 3.7 | 4 | 1.2 | 6 | 1.8 |
| Smaller Cockatoos | 16 | 4.8 | 4 | 1.2 | 6 | 1.8 |
| Larger Cockatoos | 18 | 5.5 | 5 | 1.5 | 6 | 1.8 |
| Large Macaws | 25 | 7.6 | 6 | 1.8 | 6 | 1.8 |

attached shelter unit. This may be either full-length, enabling you to walk inside easily, or raised, in which case the base is supported off the ground on legs. This is the cheaper option, as less material is needed, although it is also less flexible. Recommended flight sizes for various parrots are set out in the table above.

But it is possible to use timber for this purpose, provided that you are careful to cover it adequately. There must be no exposed edges for the parrots to gnaw at;

**Facing page:** Breeding cages for Sun and Jandaya conures. The nest boxes, food hoppers, and an automatic watering system are all exterior to the cages for ease of maintenance.

Blue-naped Parrot, *Tanygnathus lucionensis.*

lengths of timber which are at least 2 inches (5 cm) square. Treat these with a safe, non-toxic preservative, and allow this to dry thoroughly before assembling the frames. A jointed structure will be more stable, but remember to paint the cut ends as well with the preservative.

Construction of the framework should always be planned in conjunction with the width of the wire mesh which will cover it. The most popular size is probably 36 inches (90 cm) wide, although both 48-inch and 72-inch (120 and 180 cm) mesh is also available. These are more likely to sag on the framework however, unless the mesh itself is well-supported and taut on the timber framework.

otherwise they will soon start to destroy the aviary, having discovered a weakness here.

Start by ordering

A well-designed cage for a tame pet will have a door sufficiently large for easy access. A cage door hinged at the bottom forms a handy perch when open.

The individual frames need to be built so that the mesh can be attached to cover the vertical supports completely. It must also extend over the top and bottom of each unit. This ensures that when the flight is assembled, these faces, which will form the inner part of the aviary, have no exposed woodwork accessible to the parrots.

## THE AVIARY MESH

The gauge of the netting used in the construction of the flight is vital. Most species of parrot, except the smaller parrotlets, lovebirds and hanging parrots, can snip through thin 19-gauge (19 G) mesh. Thicker 16-gauge (16 G) is suitable for many other parrots, but even this may not be strong enough for the large macaws and cockatoos. Always choose square or rectangular mesh, since this will be easier to work with than the circular type.

The actual spacing between the individual strands of wire is also

The solid panels that partition this aviary into flights maximize privacy for the breeding pairs of conures housed here.

important, because if it is too wide, the parrots may destroy the aviary framework from within.

Mesh which is 1 inch (2.5 cm) square also enables mice to enter the aviary without difficulty, and these rodents are likely to prove a health hazard for the parrots.

Snakes can also be a danger in warmer climates. Breeders in

various parts of the United States and elsewhere have had valuable parrot chicks eaten by these reptiles, which gained access to the nestbox via the aviary mesh. Heavy duty chain-link fencing is sometimes used on aviaries for the larger species, but this permits the entry of rats and sparrows, which can also introduce disease to the aviary. Rats may additionally harm parrots directly.

The best solution is to use mesh which measures 1 x .5 inch (2.5 x 1.25 cm) for all parrot aviaries which are out-of-doors.

**Facing page:** As a group, *Aratinga* conures—here represented by the Jandaya—have a propensity to gnaw, so perching facilities should be conceived in terms of ease of replacement.

**Below:** Eastern Rosellas, *Platycercus eximius.*

Even if you need to use chain-link, you can construct a surrounding external framework using mesh of this size to exclude rodents. Nineteen-gauge mesh will then be quite suitable for the purpose, as it will be out of reach of the parrots themselves.

In the case of the more destructive species, do not attach the mesh directly to the wooden framework. Instead, with the assembled frame lying on a flat surface, fix a layer of .5 inch (1.25 cm) square 19 G netting around the woodwork. Take care to ensure that the cut ends

**Above:** Especially with the larger parrots, such as Pesquet's (*Psittrichas fulgidus*), care must be taken that the nest box is installed firmly.

**Facing page:** This view of a flight housing Western Rosellas (*Platycercus icterotis*) shows the landing perch and closable pophole that allows access to the shelter.

are well away from the side that will form the inner face of the flight.

You can then attach the 16-G mesh over the panels themselves, ensuring that it is positioned squarely in place; otherwise the final

**Above:** A net, with its rim well padded, is necessary to capture parrots housed in a flight, such as the Budgerigars here.

**Facing page:** The double layer of wire mesh visible here will prevent any injuries if this Turquoisine Parakeet (*Neophema pulchella*) quarrels with the occupant of the adjacent flight.

The type of mesh known as chicken wire, here supporting a Peach-faced Lovebird (*Agapornis roseicollis*) lacks durability and therefore is not ultimately economical for aviary construction.

appearance of the flight will be spoiled. The thinner mesh wrapped around the timbers ensures that the parrots will not even be able to gnaw the aviary framework through the mesh.

Netting staples, positioned every two or three inches (5-7.5 cm) around the frame, provide the most satisfactory means of attaching the mesh to the timber. Some

**Facing page:** Because these Grey Parrots' droppings and foods will fall through the mesh, cages without a solid floor have a hygienic aspect that has found favor with many parrot keepers.

Courtship display of the Red-tailed Cockatoo,
*Calyptorhynchus magnificus.*

parrots, notably Goffin's Cockatoos, are adept at removing them. Under these circumstances, heavier nails knocked flat to anchor the mesh in place around the framework are also to be advised.

In order to avoid exposing the parrots to the sharp, cut edges of the mesh, which could injure them, allow an overlap on the top and bottom of each frame of about 1 inch (2.5 cm). You should then knock this section of mesh flat, onto the adjoining face at right angles in both cases. Fix it here with netting staples, as well as on the main face. Then, once the frames are actually assembled, these particular netting staples will be out of the parrots' reach, along with the only

Peach-faced Lovebirds (*Agapornis roseicollis*) of the Normal and Blue varieties housed in an aviary featuring metal-frame construction.

sharp ends of mesh on each frame, as the sides will not have been cut in any way. In addition, the whole of the framework will be protected from the birds' beaks, once the flight is erected.

**Above:** While situating a nest box as high as possible in a flight is a good rule, it's also well to keep in mind that the male often wishes to stay nearby to guard his mate. Here the male Grey-cheeked Parakeet (*Brotogeris pyrrhopterus*) can perch atop the box.

**Facing page:** A Short-tailed Parrot, *Graydidascalus brachyurus*, housed in an aviary hygienically constructed of metal and masonry, which counters parasitic illnesses as effectively as possible.

## THE SHELTER

A solid, well-built shelter is an important

**Above:** Grey-cheeked Parakeet, *Brotogeris pyrrhopterus,* at the nest box entrance hole it has enlarged by gnawing.

part of the aviary, especially if the parrots will be living outside throughout the year. It must be dry and free from drafts, and yet light enough to encourage the birds inside, where their food will be positioned. Shelters made of bricks or concrete blocks can be

**Facing page:** Perishable foods should not be allowed to remain in the cage too long; spoiled food would present a danger to the Grey-cheeked Parakeet here.

Peach-faced Lovebird, *Agapornis roseicollis*, the wild-colored form.

framework similar to, but slightly higher than that used for the flight should be built first. The external surfaces should be covered with tongued-and-grooved wood, which creates an attractive appearance, or thick marine plywood. This needs to be used for the roof in any event.

A flat roof is the simplest type to build, with a slope running from the front nearest the shelter down to the back of the structure. Here the rainwater can be channelled away by attaching guttering. It is helpful if the roof section of the shelter is designed to fit over all the sides. This should then be covered with two layers of thick, mineralized roofing felt, extending

used for the more destructive species, but they are costly.

Again, a wooden shelter is suitable for most smaller parrots, providing that it is constructed with thought beforehand. A

Alexandrine Parakeets, *Psittacula eupatria,* in an aviary furnished with a tree branch for perching.

Peach-faced Lovebird, *Agapornis roseicollis*, the color variety called Blue.

tempered hardboard, which can be wiped over quite easily, making it especially useful in aviaries housing nectar-feeding parrots. But these lining materials are vulnerable to the birds' beaks, and any rodents which gain access to the aviary.

It will therefore be important to protect all edges adequately with thick hardwood battening. This will need to be replaced at intervals as it is gnawed away. Alternatively, you can use metal strips for this purpose, but it is vital to ensure they are flush with the lining material. Otherwise, the parrots could become caught up here, or could slice their toes on a sharp edge of metal.

down onto the side as necessary, to prevent drafts and damp penetration here.

The interior of the shelter may be lined with thin plywood or oil-

A group of Lesser Sulphur-crested Cockatoos (*Cacatua sulphurea*) clinging to the aviary wire. Nervous parrots will characteristically retreat to the upper rear of their enclosure.

A pair of Abyssinian Lovebirds, *Agapornis taranta*.

otherwise they may build a nest behind a solid lining. Obviously however, there is less insulation in the shelter with a lining of this type. Seed husks and other dirt accumulating on or behind the mesh can also be difficult to remove.

You will need to include at least one window at the rear of the shelter. This is conveniently located in the door. It must be wired over with mesh so that the parrots do not attempt to fly into the glass and hurt themselves. It will be useful if this particular window is removable, so that ventilation in the shelter can be improved on hot days. You may also decide to include another window in one of the sides as well.

Another possibility is simply to wire over with mesh all exposed surfaces in the shelter. This ensures there will be nowhere for rodents to hide, if they enter the shelter, whereas

A trio of Sun Conures (*Aratinga solstitialis*) enjoying the sunlight, a benefit of having a portion of the flight roofed only with wire.

**Facing page:** Aerial view of an aviary, showing how the solid roof covering the shelter extends over part of the flight as well.

**Right:** In the wild, many parrots nest in tree-trunk cavities, a circumstance duplicated here for Malee Ringneck Parrots, *Barnardius barnardi macgillivrayi.*

Around the entry door to the shelter, you will probably want to include a safety porch. This is a simple structure, made in an identical fashion to the flight, except of course there will be an entrance door here. This needs to open outwards, giving easy access to the interior.

The purpose of this safety porch is to prevent any birds escaping when you enter the aviary. You will therefore have to close the door in the safety porch behind you, before opening the entry door to the shelter. From here, you will need a third door, leading from the shelter into the flight itself. Alternatively, you can have another entrance, and separate safety porch attached to the flight. If you plan only one means of entry to the aviary however, this should be via the shelter, since it is here the parrots will need to be fed and watered every day. This also means that you will not disturb the parrots

View looking through a series of flights housing South American parrots. A Black-headed Caique (*Pionites melanocephala*) is perched on an artificial tree.

Fischer's Lovebird, *Agapornis fischeri.*

when they are breeding in the flight.

## ASSEMBLY

The site for the aviary will need to be marked out carefully, and levelled as necessary before assembly starts. The whole structure should be mounted on a layer of block work, or bricks, extending at least 12 inches (30 cm) below the surface of the ground, and for a similar height above. This will support the aviary and should prevent it from rotting prematurely. In addition, secure foundations also help to discourage vermin from burrowing into the flight, even if a grass floor is used here.

The shelter should have a concrete base however, about 4 inches (10 cm) thick, under which a layer of aviary netting covering this floor can be incorporated, to exclude rats. A basic damp course is also advisable, and a layer of heavy duty polyethylene sheeting

**Facing page:** One of the more distinctive parrot species, Hawk-headed Parrots (*Deroptyus accipitrinus*) here occupy a spacious outdoor aviary.

Masked Lovebird, *Agapornis personata*, the wild coloration.

should be set above the netting for this purpose.

Bolts can be used to hold the frames to the base. They should be set upright in the mortar between the bricks or blocks. This must then be left to dry thoroughly, before you start to assemble the frames. You will need to drill corresponding holes in the woodwork to accommodate the bolts. Then oil the bolts, before fastening washers and nuts in place.

Once the frames have been assembled by this means, you will then be able to add further mortar around the base to give additional support to the structure. Masonry nails driven through the wood into the brickwork beneath will also be useful.

## THE FLIGHT FLOOR

The vast majority of parrots, except perhaps the hanging parrots, will destroy any plants growing within their enclosure, and so parrot

Citron-crested Cockatoo, the most strongly colored form of the Lesser Sulphur-crested Cockatoo, *Cacatua sulphurea.*

aviaries often appear rather bare. Grass floors are attractive at first, but muddy patches soon develop and the ground becomes fouled, especially in relatively small flights.

In a larger area, where there is space for gravel paths, grass can be a more satisfactory covering. You will need to include areas of concrete under the perches, where the majority of droppings will accumulate, and clean these off regularly. Although parrots, especially cockatoos, will spend time on a grass floor, it will be otherwise hard to clean properly,

When evaluating types of aviary flooring, hygiene should be taken into consideration. The parrot housed here is the Hispaniolan Amazon, *Amazona ventralis*.

Masked Lovebird, *Agapornis personata*, the blue mutation.

another possible covering. Again, concrete bases beneath the perches are to be recommended for cleanliness. There is a risk that rats could tunnel up into the aviary however, so it may be worthwhile including a suitable layer of mesh, before spreading the gravel over the floor.

Concrete or paving slabs are other practical alternatives, especially for aviaries housing nectar-feeding parrots, which have relatively liquid droppings. Such floor coverings can be scraped or hosed off regularly, and even disinfected easily as required. A simple drainage system

leading to an increased risk of infections. Parasitic worms can also become established easily in these surroundings.

A deep bed of coarse gravel, at least 6 inches (15 cm) in thickness is

**Facing page:**
In this communal aviary, Roseringed Parakeets *(Psittacula krameri)* and Cockatiels coexist with doves.

which need not consist of more than a slope running towards the end of the flight away from the shelter, will cope with heavy rainfall which would completely saturate grass. You must include a mesh grid or small pipe in the brickwork at the lowest point, so water can then drain out of the flight, without admitting mice.

## PERCHES

The parrots will prefer perches cut to fit across the aviary. These are easier to attach by wire looped around the end of the flight. Cut branches from trees which have not

A party of Blue-crowned Conures, *Aratinga acuticaudata*, photographed in the wild in Argentina.

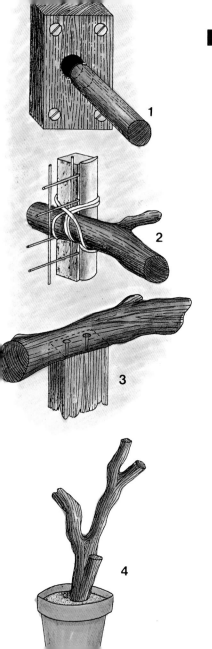

been recently sprayed with chemicals and are known to be safe for parrots. Sycamore and apple are popular choices for the purpose, as is elder, although this will be destroyed quickly. Yew and laburnum are likely to be poisonous, while privet and lilac are similarly dangerous for use as perches.

All branches should be washed off thoroughly before being placed in the

1. For smaller parrot species, dowel perches can be attached to the walls of the cage.

2. Branches should be installed in a fashion that allows easy replacement.

3. Branch attached to an upright to form a T-shaped perch.

4. A free-standing perch consisting of a branch set into a flower pot.

Perches notched to be slipped onto cage wire:

—the natural shape offers the parrot's foot a variety of grips

—turned to a cylinder allows easy cleaning

—sandpaper covers will help to keep the claws of some parrots trimmed

aviary. You can make heavier lengths into 'T'-shape perches for large species such as macaws, and fix these into the floor of the aviary, or into a secure pot. Dowelling is suitable for the smaller parrots and often used in the shelter. But you must provide a constant supply of natural branches. This will help to keep the birds' feet in good condition, and enables them to use their beaks. Parrots enjoy stripping bark off their perches, and

Tame parrots, such as this Sulphur-crested Cockatoo (*Cacatua galerita*) will enjoy spending time on a playground, outside the cage.

this in turn keeps them occupied. They will concentrate on attacking accessible branches, which diverts their attention away from the wooden framework of the

weather in the outside flight. You should therefore attach lengths of white flat or corrugated plastic sheeting on the roof here, nearest to the shelter. It will need to extend for 4 feet (120 cm), and for a similar distance on the sides. White is preferable, because it reflects the summer heat.

Many parrots will roost in their nestbox at night through the year. It can be located under the covered part of the flight for the summer months, when the parrots will hopefully be breeding. During the winter period, the nestbox should be transferred to the interior of the shelter, so the parrots will roost inside. If allowed to remain on an exposed perch, they may lose toes from frost-bite.

aviary itself.

## CLIMATIC CONSIDERATIONS

Even established parrots will need some protection from bad

Cuban Amazon, *Amazona leucocephala.*

damage the kidneys irreversibly, and lead to a slow death from nephrosis. You can provide heat in the shelter by means of an electrical heater. This is the safest way of heating the structure. Add a thermostat to the circuitry to minimize the cost, and take care to ensure that all wiring and the heating itself will be adequately protected from the parrots in a mesh cage.

This also applies to lighting fittings, but a light will only be necessary if the birds have to be fed when it would normally be dark. In this case, a time-switch working a low wattage bulb can be pre-set, so that the light comes on, just before you go into the aviary. The parrots will

Even though parrots are hardy once acclimatized, exposure to very low temperatures should be avoided. Excess cold can

A tame Moluccan Cockatoo (*Cacatua moluccensis*) enjoys having its head scratched, for this resembles the preening it would receive from a mate of its own species.

not then be panicked when you open the aviary door, as they will find the perches easily in the light, rather than flying around wildly.

## EXPANSION

If you want a number of aviaries, it is preferable to build a range of flight units, and connect them by a service corridor, running behind the indoor quarters. It is vital to ensure that both sides of the adjoining framework are clad with mesh however, because otherwise, the parrots will bite each other's toes. This can cause serious injury, which is totally preventable by double-wiring the frames.

Try to arrange any new construction work for the early fall, after the breeding season. The disturbance to the existing birds will be minimal, and they can be released back into their quarters before the weather turns cold. If you are being troubled with cats climbing onto the aviary, now is also a good time to take further precautions for the following year. Fix an additional layer of thin 22 gauge 2 inch (5 cm) mesh over the outer surface of the roof. This should help to deter them from settling down here and disturbing the birds beneath.

Since a perch is a familiar object to a caged parrot, this Grey Parrot will step onto the perch, and it then can be removed from the cage.

# *Feeding Parrots*

For many years, parrots were expected to survive and breed on a diet often limited to little more than sunflower seed, sometimes with a few peanuts added. In the wild, of course, dried seeds are a rarity for most parrots. They eat ripening fruit and seeds, greenstuff, nuts, and

Seed mixtures, often incorporating sunflower, have traditionally been the basic food for most parrot species. They can be offered sprouted (below) to those species whose diet naturally includes a large proportion of soft foods—such as the family of Cobalt-winged Parakeets (*Brotogeris cyanoptera*, facing page).

sometimes even insects. Lories, lorikeets, and hanging parrots also consume pollen and nectar as a regular part of their diet. This particular group of parrots have more specialist feeding habits, although their needs can be met quite adequately with the range of substitute diets which are now available. You can in fact obtain specially formulated foods for all parrots, and this has helped greatly to improve breeding results.

Fruits and vegetables can be served in with the seed mixture (below); however, many parrots (such as the Peach-faced Lovebird on the facing page) will preferentially consume seeds to the exclusion of the soft foods available.

## THE FOOD ELEMENTS

The basic ingredients of fat, carbohydrate, and protein are common to all foods. But the actual composition of foodstuffs varies, so that in practical terms, feeding one type of seed should help to compensate for deficiences in another. The cereal group, for example, contains more carbohydrate than oil-based seeds. But these in turn are a more valuable source of both fat and protein, as the accompanying table shows.

Carbohydrate is used by the body as a source of energy. If there is an excess, it can be converted and stored in the body as fat. It can then be utilized for energy later if necessary. Fat itself is also

| Seed | Percentage Food Value | | |
|---|---|---|---|
| | **Carbohydrate** | **Oil** | **Protein** |
| Canary Seed | 55 | 4 | 16 |
| Millet | 56 | 5 | 14 |
| Maize | 70 | 4 | 9 |
| Oats | 60 | 6 | 12 |
| Sunflower | 20 | 47 | 24 |
| Peanut Kernels | 19 | 47 | 26 |
| Pine Nuts | 12 | 47 | 31 |
| Hemp | 17 | 40 | 22 |

(Samples can vary according to age, growing and storage conditions, etc.)

With larger parrots—such at this Sulphur-crested Cockatoo, *Cacatua galerita*—to prevent spillage, food is best offered in heavy-weight utensils made of ceramic or metal.

important to protect the body organs against trauma. Protein is particularly significant for growth, and during the molting period, when new feathers are being produced.

Protein is made up of individual amino-acid units, and the actual proportions vary according to the individual protein. Some amino acids can be manufactured in the body by the liver, but others need to be present in the diet. There are about 20 amino acids, and of these, up to half may be essential to parrots. They

have to be present in the protein of parrots' food, otherwise a deficiency will arise.

Most cereal and oil seeds are low in sulphur—containing methionine, as well as lysine. These amino-acids are especially important in the development of

**Above:** A Cockatiel and a Peach-fronted Conure (*Aratinga aurea*) on a playground fitted with stainless-steel food dishes.

**Facing page:** Millet sprays clipped to the cage provide a Cockatiel or other parrot with occupation as well as nutrition.

plumage. A deficiency of lysine, for example, may cause abnormal coloration of feathering. Odd areas of yellow plumage are often apparent in imported parrots, such as Blue-fronted Amazons. This can arise because the lack of lysine in their diet

**Above:** Commercially available products for parrots include items such as vitamin supplements (left) and protection against parasites (right).

**Facing page:** A Lutino Cockatiel in a cage fitted with food and water dishes that can be replenished from the outside. Ground corn cob is used to cover the cage tray.

A pet Finsch's Conure, *Aratinga finschi,* housed in a planted enclosure.

**Facing page:** Introduction to the varied diet necessary to keep a parrot healthy is best done while the bird is still young. This hand-tame Grey Parrot is willing to sample whatever is offered it.

interferes with the development of the normal green pigmentation, creating yellow rather than green feathering. Such changes are usually only temporary, and will be reversed at the next molt, providing the parrot's diet is improved.

Aside from water, there are also two other important ingredients of food, in the form of minerals and vitamins. Minerals and the related trace elements (which are present at much lower levels) are vital for many

As with these Budgerigars, greenfood such as chickweed can be offered occasionally to vary the diet.

biological reactions in the body. They are also important elsewhere—in the skeleton for example, where calcium and phosphorus are vital for a healthy bone structure. Breeding hens require increased amounts of calcium, to compensate for that lost from the body via eggshells, which are comprised largely of calcium carbonate. Mineral deficiencies may lead to general weakness and lack of condition. Breeding results will be persistently poor, and there can be a high incidence of soft-shelled eggs if calcium is in short supply.

Vitamins are only required in small quantities, but they are of great importance to the parrot's health. These compounds are often divided into two groups, known as fat-soluble and water-soluble vitamins. Those in the first category, comprising vitamins A, D3, E and K are stored in the body, unlike vitamin C and members of the vitamin B complex. Vitamins must generally be present in the food to avoid deficiency diseases, although some, such as vitamins C and K, can be made by parrots if necessary.

There is a danger following prolonged use of antibiotics that the beneficial bacteria which synthesize vitamins may be adversely affected. For this reason, a supplement is usually given at this stage. In addition, recently-imported birds may be deficient in certain

Food and water utensils that can be replenished from outside the flight minimize the disturbances that can hinder breeding.

vitamins if they have received an inadequate diet. Nectar-feeding parrots and the Eclectus, for example, may suffer from a shortage of vitamin A, which gives rise to the disease candidiasis. Again, supplementation is a useful precaution when you first obtain such birds.

## CEREALS

Millet and canary seed form the basis of feeding mixes for smaller species such as parrotlets. Millets of various types are grown throughout most of the warmer areas of the world. Millet sprays (seedheads) are popular with many species, while loose panicum millet, along with pearl white and other strains are included in a mixture of millets.

Canary seed tends to be slightly more brownish than millet, and can also be distinguished by its shape. It is oval, with pointed ends, rather than round. Quantities of canary seed are grown in North Africa, especially Morocco, and elsewhere, including Argentina, Canada and the United States. As with millet, choose a mixed blend, since this will compensate for deficiencies which may be present in one growing area. Offer a mix of both millets and canary seed as well, because although these cereals are low in lysine, they tend to supplement each other with regard to other essential amino acids.

Maize often features in parrot seed mixtures for larger birds. It may be present in the form of flakes, or "kibbled," meaning that it is broken into pieces. The seed itself

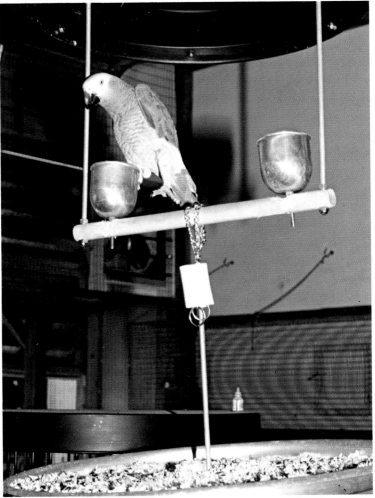

Tame parrots like this Grey Parrot will be quite content to spend the day on an open perch, provided food and water are available.

is hardy and relatively large, so only parrots with powerful beaks, such as macaws, can eat it easily. As with corn-on-the-cob however, maize can be cooked (do not add any salt), and this will tenderize it. Newly-imported and young parrots will eagerly consume these cereals in this form. Always allow the maize to cool down after cooking; otherwise it may burn the parrot's mouth. Also, as with soaked seed, cooked maize becomes a perishable foodstuff, and must be removed daily, before it can turn moldy.

Oats have a higher oil content than other cereal crops, and a relatively low energy value. They are a fairly thin, narrow seed, sometimes included in cheap seed mixtures, but are often discarded by the birds. In contrast, dehulled oats, which are called groats, and are pale yellow in color, are usually readily consumed.

There are two other cereals which may form part of a parrot mix. Sorghum is a popular crop in dry areas because of its drought-resistant properties, and is grown as an alternative to maize in certain parts of North America. It contains more protein and less oil than maize, with two non-saccharine strains being marketed as milo and kafir. While parrots will eat this quite readily in

**Facing page:** A Scaly-headed, or Maximilian's, Parrot (*Pionus maximiliani*) in a cage of the type commonly used to house pet parrots.

many cases, this does not apply to paddy rice. A small, yellowish, flattened seed, it is most suitable for parrotlets and lovebirds. But even Madagascar Lovebirds, which are said to feed on this seed in their homeland, rarely accept paddy rice in captivity.

## OIL SEEDS

Sunflower seed forms the basis of most standard parrot mixtures. White, striped and black varieties are available, but especially in Europe, black sunflower is not popular because it is said to contain a toxic factor, especially if it is soaked in water. In nutritional terms, white sunflower is preferable, as it contains a relatively higher level of protein and is lower in oil than striped seeds. Unfortunately, the yield is also lower, so that it proves more costly. You can purchase it separately however, should you so wish, for use during the breeding season, for example.

Peanuts are fed to parrots either loose or still in their pods. They are also called groundnuts because the nuts actually develop underground, after the flowers have been fertilized in the air. Always store them, like other seed, in dry surroundings, because otherwise they are likely to develop a lethal mold. Groundnuts contaminated in this way were first identified as a cause of death in birds in 1961. The aflatoxins produced by the *Aspergillus* mold will

The potential of the Grey Parrot as a talker has spread its fame throughout the world. Here two Greys are fancifully portrayed in an Oriental style, feeding in a flowering tree.

give rise to severe liver damage over a period of time

Various other nuts are sometimes added to parrot mixes, especially for larger birds. These can include brazils, which are easily cracked by the powerful beaks of macaws, as well as walnuts and hazelnuts. Their availability tends to be seasonal, and if they are not stocked by your pet store, you may be able to obtain them from a health food store. Incidentally, never be tempted to feed salted nuts sold for human consumption to parrots, as these will be harmful.

Pine nuts are less widely available than sunflower seed, and the supply may be sporadic. This is because they are collected from the wild, in the coniferous forests of Eastern Europe and China. The smaller grades are suitable for all parrots, whereas the larger nuts should be offered only to bigger species which can crack their shells. Pine nuts resemble hazelnuts in taste, and are usually eaten very readily by parrots.

On occasions, some batches of pine nuts may be contaminated with a bluish-green mold. This will be noticeable on any chipped nuts, and they should not be offered to the parrots, as they are likely to prove harmful.

Other oil seeds are occasionally included in parrot food mixtures, notably hemp. But the sale of this round, dark seed is restricted in some areas because of its drug connections. It is

**Facing page:** Red-capped Parrots, *Purpureicephalus spurius.*

especially valuable for feeding in cold weather, but do restrict the quantity on offer. It can be fattening, and parrots will often gorge themselves on hemp in preference to other seeds.

## SEED DIETS FOR PARROTS

At your local pet store, you will find suitable prepared parrot mixes available. Alternatively, you can purchase the individual seeds and make up your own mixture. The figures in the accompanying table below will help in this regard, but do remember that parrots have individual tastes. What suits one bird may not be relished by another.

If a parrot does decide to scatter its seed everywhere while seeking

**Facing page:** White-capped Parrot, *Pionus senilis*.

| | Sunflower | Pine Nuts | Peanuts | Millet | Canary | Other |
|---|---|---|---|---|---|---|
| Lovebirds/ Parrotlets, etc. | 1 | - | - | 2 | 3 | Spray millet, hemp |
| Medium-sized Parrots, e.g. *Pionus, Poicephalus* | 3 | 2 | $^1/_2$ | $^1/_2$ | $^1/_2$ | Spray Millet Groundnuts in shell |
| Larger Parrots, Macaws & Cockatoos | 3 | 2 | 1 | $^1/_2$ | $^1/_2$ | Brazil and other nuts may be popular, Chilies |

a favorite item, it may prove more economical to offer at least some of the seeds separately. You can provide the smaller cereal seeds in an individual pot. Otherwise, they may sink to the bottom in among larger seeds, and the parrot will have difficulty in picking them out.

When buying seed from your pet store, check that it is clean. Sealed packets or bags are preferable to seed in open containers, which may have been contaminated by dirt and dust in the environment. Avoid storing seed at home in sealed plastic bags or sacks. This can lead to condensation on the inside, which causes the seed to begin germinating, and then turn moldy. In addition, as with paper sacks,

rodents will have easy access to seed kept in this way. Most breeders prefer to use metal seed bins or tins for storage purposes, located in a cool, dry environment.

## DIETS FOR NECTAR-FEEDING PARROTS

Early recipes were often based largely on milk and sponge cake or biscuits, and this group of parrots gained a reputation for succumbing with fits. In fact, lories and lorikeets are almost exclusively dependent on pollen and nectar collected from flowering plants, and a similar substitute must

**Facing page:** For these Red Lories (*Eos bornea*) orange halves have been impaled on the perch. The tree trunk nearby contains a hole for nesting.

always be offered to aviary birds as well as fruit, if they are to remain healthy. The difference in their dietary needs is apparent by studying their digestive system. The walls of their gizzards for example, where food is broken down, are much less muscular than those of seed-eating parrots.

There are now various special proprietary foods available for nectar-feeding parrots. These simply need to be mixed with water in the required proportions. Be sure that the solution is not hot however, as this could burn the birds' tongues. If you decide to change from one brand of nectar to another, do this gradually, so as to not upset the birds' digestive systems. The latest innovation in the care of nectar-feeding parrots is the use of dry powders, which are sprinkled over fruit. These are similar in their formulation to fluid feeds, but avoid the need for the parrots to consume what is usually an abnormally large volume of water as part of their diet.

Seed, especially soaked millet sprays, can be offered to lories and lorikeets, but it should not become the major item in their diet. Hanging parrots appear to take more seed than these other nectar-feeders, and will even eat a softbill food on a regular basis.

**Facing page:** A Canary-winged Parakeet, *Brotogeris versicolorus*. The shape of the bill suggests that birds of this genus feed extensively on soft foods.

## FRUIT AND GREENSTUFF

Fruit of various types should be offered to parrots every day, although some birds may be reluctant to sample it at first. The choice on offer will depend to some extent on where you live, and the depth of your pocket! Sweet apple is a useful standby, being widely available and popular with most species. Grapes also are usually acceptable.

There is virtually no restriction on the selection of fruit which you can use, although citrus fruits such as orange are perhaps too acid. You can even use canned fruit, preferably in natural juice rather than syrup, although this should be drained off in any event.

Choose only good quality fresh fruits; damaged bananas and over-ripe pears are certainly not to be recommended.

It is probably better to dice large fruits into pieces. These will be easier for the parrots to eat, and can be given in a suitable pot. Always wash the fruit thoroughly beforehand. Some parrot-keepers also remove the skin, as a precaution against chemical residues here, which may result from sprays or storage conditions. Carrots, which are a valuable source of Vitamin A, should always be peeled before being offered to the parrots.

Greenstuff is also appreciated by many

**Facing page:** Red-rumped Parrot, *Psephotus haematonotus*, a male.

Three pet parrots—two Cockatiels and a Yellow-headed Amazon (*Amazona ochrocephala*)—watch as the soft-food portion of their diet is prepared.

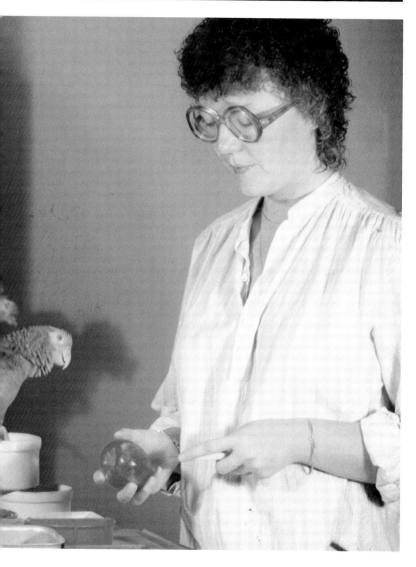

parrots. Spinach beet is easily cultivated in most gardens, and ensures a fresh uncontaminated supply for much of the year. Wild plants such as chickweed are also popular, with plantain seed-heads and seeding grasses being useful for smaller species later in the year. Some parrots will take berries, such as blackberries, and even ripe, orange rose hips will be eaten. Certain birds prefer the rose seeds, while others eat the outer hull.

If you collect wild foods however, then you must be absolutely certain that they have not been contaminated by chemical spraying, or fouled in any other way. Avoid roadside verges, since vegetation here, apart

from possibly being sprayed, is also likely to show raised lead levels from exhaust fumes. Always wash such foods as well, as a further precaution against harming your stock.

If you have a number of parrots, it may be worthwhile freezing quantities of fresh foods for use later in the year. Peas, beans and corn-on-the-cob may all be stored satisfactorily in this way, as can grapes. You can then thaw out required amounts for feeding to your parrots over the winter months, when supplies are likely to be more expensive.

**Facing page:** Eastern Rosella, *Platycercus eximius.*

## FOOD PREPARATION

Apart from basic seed mixes, most other food for parrots will need to be prepared fresh every day. If you choose to offer soaked seed, you will need a separate bowl, in which the required amount of seed can be immersed in water for a day. This process stimulates germination, causing the protein and Vitamin B levels of the seed to rise as a result. Soaked seed is especially valuable for breeding stock, since it can be more easily digested by the chicks.

Millet sprays are popular for this purpose, but sunflower seed and mung beans can also be used satisfactorily. Mung beans can also be sprouted, using a kit available from health food stores. In both cases however, you must wash the seed off very thoroughly under a running tap, and allow it to drain, before feeding it to the birds. As with other fresh foods, soaked seed will turn moldy, and will be injurious to their health if it is left in their quarters for more than a day. Try to measure the quantity accurately, so there is no wastage, and remove any uneaten soaked seed at the end of each day. Most parrots prefer seed in this form, so that they will usually eat it before dry seed.

A fresh supply of nectar must also be given each day. In hot surroundings,

**Facing page:** Blue-winged Parrotlet, *Forpus xanthopterygius.*

it may be preferable to provide a smaller volume, mixed fresh in the morning and late afternoon. Hygiene is particularly important with this group of parrots. Under no circumstances should you add a new solution of nectar to the previous one, because this can lead to serious digestive upsets and even losses.

Similarly with greenfood and fruit, any remaining should be removed before it can turn moldy. It is preferable to feed the parrots in the shelter. Here, if the floor is lined with newspaper, then it will be quite easy to clean up any spilt perishable foods, simply by replacing the sheets. Since some parrots will chew up

paper, avoid using colored sheets, in case these contain toxic inks.

You can obtain from your local pet store a variety of suitable containers for feeding parrots. For the larger species, choose stainless steel or ceramic pots, since these will not be destroyed as easily as plastic containers. Special sealed drinkers are most suitable for water, as they are less likely to be fouled by food or droppings. These drinkers may need to be attached through aviary mesh, in which case they can be suspended on a side of the flight.

During cold weather, you must check that the water in the spout of such containers has not frozen. This can happen although

The Orange-winged Amazon, *Amazona amazonica,* is one of the most extensively imported of the amazons.

the water in the bottle remains liquid. Never fill these containers to the brim during the winter, because they are likely to crack as the water expands on freezing.

Nectar should never be given in open pots, because it will attract insects, which could prevent the birds from feeding, or even sting them. In addition, the parrot's plumage will become soiled as it feeds, dipping its head into the container. Some lories will even try to bathe in a pot of nectar, with catastrophic consequences.

**Facing page:** A pair of Grey-cheeked Parakeets, *Brotogeris pyrrhopterus*. Proper diet is essential if parrots are to come into breeding condition.

Plastic drinkers with an open spout, rather than those with a ball-valve design are most suitable for nectar. They are reasonably durable, and easy to clean with a bottle-brush. If you buy at least two containers, then you can rotate them, washing one to replace the other. Containers for nectar must be kept spotlessly clean, with no chips or cracks where bacteria and fungi could thrive. A separate drinker of water only must also be provided for all nectar-feeders.

Containers which hook onto the aviary mesh should be located by a perch under cover, so their contents remain dry and are less likely to be scattered when the parrots alight to feed.

Some birds may prefer to eat off the shelter floor, and the heavy ceramic pots, (as sold for dogs), are ideal for macaws.

For less destructive species, you can build a feeding table on a solid base, fitting a rim around the top to prevent the food being spilled. If this top is removable, it can be easily washed off, making it particularly valuable for use with nectar-feeders. Since heavy dishes are hard for parrots to overturn, they ensure that food wastage is kept to a minimum.

## GRIT AND MINERALS

Seed-eating birds generally require a source of grit to assist with the digestion of their food. For parrots, a mixture of mineralized and oyster shell grit is to be recommended. Smaller species tend to visit the grit pot more regularly than their larger counterparts, and it should be topped up weekly. Budgerigar grit is suitable for lovebirds and other parrots of similar size, but pigeon grit may be more satisfactory for larger species. Grit will gradually dissolve away in the acid environment of the gizzard, where it helps to break down the food. As it dissolves, so grit will supplement the parrot's mineral requirement.

Cuttlefish bone is also an important source of minerals, containing a

**Facing page:** A cuttlefish bone is the easiest way to supplement a parrot's diet with calcium and other minerals.

high percentage of calcium as well as other minerals, including magnesium. Minute quantities of copper, aluminum and further assorted trace elements are also present here. Larger amounts of cuttlefish bone are likely to be consumed during the breeding season, but always offer a supply throughout the year, with the soft, powdery side accessible to the parrots.

You can buy cuttlefish bone and special clips to hold them in place from your pet store. If you come across any bones washed up on the beach, be careful not to take home any which are oiled or otherwise discolored. Provided they are quite clean, cuttlefish bones can be washed off and left to soak in a bucket of water for at least a week. Change the water daily, and give them a final rinse. Then the bones can be left to dry off thoroughly in the sun, or indoors, before being stored for use.

## FOOD SUPPLEMENTS

Tonics of various kinds have been marketed for many years to provide an additional intake of vitamins and minerals. Now however, you can obtain comprehensive products intended and formulated specially for birds. These are usually available in powder form,

**Facing page:** The Senegal Parrot, *Poicephalus senegalus*, is the best known member of this African parrot genus.

and easily administered by being sprinkled over fruit or greenstuff.

Dry seed is less satisfactory, because the powder tends to be lost, simply accumulating in the bottom of the food pot, rather than sticking to the seed. Choose a supplement which contains essential amino acids, as well as vitamins and minerals, even though this will tend to be more expensive. Ask at your pet store for advice about the available brands.

The other major advance in feeding parrots is the introduction of pelleted diets. These are again specially prepared for this purpose, containing the known essential ingredients to keep the birds in good health, and encourage breeding activity. There are both breeding rations, intended to be fed at breeding time and maintenance diets available.

The drawback of pellets is the reluctance of some parrots to eat them. You can mix pellets in among dry seed, in the hope of persuading the birds to sample them. It is much easier with hand-raised parrots however, since they may already be used to pelleted food, and are naturally more adventurous in their feeding habits.

Even if pellets become the staple diet of your

**Facing page:** Major Mitchéll's, or Leadbeater's, Cockatoo, *Cacatua leadbeateri.*

parrots, you should continue to offer fruit and similar foods. Pet parrots in particular can become bored with pellets, and may decide to crunch them up, which can be very wasteful. Always be sure that drinking water is freely available, since parrots on a pelleted diet tend to drink more than those eating seed.

## RODENTS

Wherever seed and other foodstuffs are accessible out-of-doors, there is a possibility that rodents will be attracted to the area. Mice and rats can become a major problem in aviaries if they gain access, by eating seed and disturbing the birds. They also represent a considerable disease hazard, capable of transmitting various diseases such as salmonellosis, to which parrots are susceptible. Infections of this type often prove fatal, following ingestion of contaminated food.

Spring traps and poisons are too dangerous for use in an aviary alongside birds, but you may be able to place them safely on the floor of a parrot cage located in the aviary. Provided that the door is securely closed, only the rodents should be able to enter via the gaps between the cage bars.

Alternatively, you can now obtain traps which catch mice alive, and these can usually be placed within the aviary itself. They have the added advantage of being able to

A young Cockatiel (*Nymphicus hollandicus*) of the Pearl variety.

take a number of rodents at one setting, so it should be possible to eliminate a population quite quickly.

If all else fails, it may be necessary to remove the parrots, particularly if rats are involved. These, unlike mice, are liable to harm the birds directly, and may kill them. Seek the advice of a rodent control company.

The only other option which you have available is the use of sulphur fuses. First, you will need to establish the whereabouts of all the exits from the rats' tunnels. They may be located outside the aviary, hidden by long grass or other vegetation. Block these off, using damp cloths held in place with bricks, and place the lit fuses down the main opening before sealing this as well. The sulphur gas should kill all the rats quickly and effectively in their burrows.

This group of feeding lories includes Rainbows *(Trichoglossus haematodus)* and Violet-necks *(Eos squamata).*

# *Breeding Parrots*

Major advances have taken place in the breeding of parrots during the last decade, and part of the reason for this trend is the ease with which pairs can be recognized. Better nutrition has also played a part, both by encouraging the parrots to nest in the first instance, and by facilitating hand-raising of their chicks.

The use of incubators has also become more widespread. As a result, it is possible to remove eggs shortly after laying, so the chicks can be hatched and

reared separately. By this stage, the adult parrots should be nesting again. This system, often called "double clutching," actually stimulates the parrots' natural reproductive cycle, and can obviously double the number of chicks produced in a breeding season.

## SEXING PARROTS

Discovering if you have a true pair used to be a major problem when trying to breed parrots, although some species, such as Eclectus, can be easily sexed by their appearance. South American parrots in contrast can rarely be

**Facing page:** The Galah, or Roseate Cockatoo (*Eolophus roseicapillus*).

distinguished by this means. For many years, breeders had to rely largely on luck when selecting a pair. They looked to the shape of the head, size of the beak and other physical attributes to distinguish the sexes.

Such pointers can be useful indicators in some cases. Cock macaws, for example, often have broader heads and larger nostrils than hens, but this is not a foolproof method of identification. The multi-colored macaws range from Central America southward, and occurring over such a wide area, there is often a natural variation in size, irrespective of the birds' gender.

Behavioral observations may also assist in sexing such birds, but again, these are not infallible. Although a pair may preen each other's plumage, so will two individuals of the same sex when they are kept together. In the cases of the hanging parrots and lovebirds, which regularly build nests (unlike most psittacines), hens alone are usually responsible for this activity, but it is not a conclusive sign because a cock bird may occasionally undertake the task.

At the end of the last century, breeders became aware of a varying gap between the pelvic bones. These can be felt as hard swellings just above the

**Facing page:** A Blue-winged Parakeet (*Neophema chrysostoma*) feeding young at the entrance of the nest cavity.

vent. As a result, the so-called "pelvic bone test" became popular for sexing parrots which showed no plumage differences. Unfortunately, this space is only wider when the hen is about to lay, assisting in the passage of eggs. Outside the breeding season, or with immature birds, it gives unreliable results, indicating a high proportion of cock birds. There is no fixed scale of measurements available for the various species

**Above:** A six-week-old Rose-ringed Parakeet, *Psittacula krameri.*

**Facing page:** Parrot chicks a few weeks old: Rose-ringed Parakeets (*Psittacula krameri*) and Yellow-naped Macaws (*Ara auricollis*).

either, and decisions are taken by means of comparison only.

The most popular method of sexing parrots today is known as surgical sexing. The bird is anesthetized, so that a small incision can be

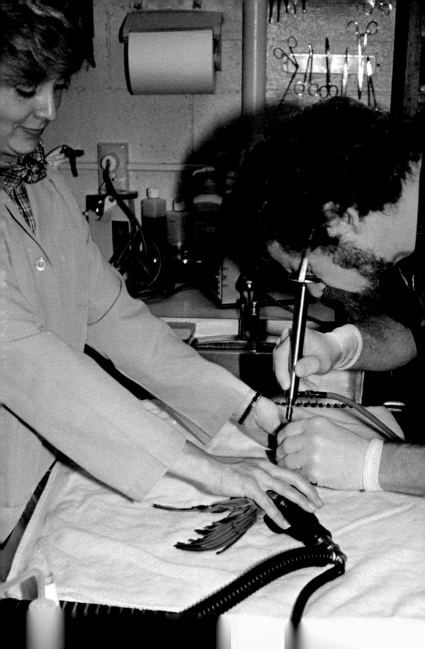

made in the abdomen. Then, using an endoscope, it is possible for the veterinarian to look directly at the parrot's reproductive organs. This method is therefore very reliable and safe in experienced hands. Other information, such as the reproductive state of a hen's ovaries can be gleaned by this technique, and it is only unsatisfactory in immature parrots.

In this instance, the laboratory method of chromosomal karyotyping can be used. Starting with a tiny blood sample, obtained from a plucked feather, it is then possible to construct a chromosome map which shows all the paired chromosomes found in the nucleus of every living cell in the body. There is one pair of chromosomes, called the sex chromosomes, which differ in appearance between the sexes. Hen birds have one of the chromosomes of this pair much shorter than the other.

By studying the magnified karyotype, it is possible to sex the parrot, having discovered the sex chromosomes. If there is no difference in their length, then the bird is a cock. Since there are no ratios involved, the method is usually reliable. But you may have difficulty in finding a laboratory which carries

**Facing page:** A veterinarian viewing the reproductive glands of an anesthetized conure through an endoscope.

out this service commercially, depending on where you live.

Compatibility is another significant factor in the successful breeding of parrots. Simply because you have two parrots of opposite sex does not necessarily mean that they will prove compatible and keen to nest. This applies

A Yellow-naped Macaw (*Ara auricollis*) and a Blue-crowned Conure (*Aratinga acuticaudata*), both a few weeks old.

These ten-week-old youngsters are hybrids between two species of *Pionus* parrots, the Blue-headed (*P. menstruus*) and the White-capped (*P. senilis*).

especially with regard to the larger species, where a new mate may not be readily accepted.

Unfortunately, the cost of most bigger parrots does not permit a number of one species to be purchased, and left until they form into individual pairs. Then, a further problem may arise with unpaired birds, because most parrots must be kept separately for breeding purposes; otherwise they may fight, with devastating results.

## NESTBOXES

Parrots occasionally choose to lay in the strangest of places. Some even prefer to rear their chicks on the floor of an aviary, rather than using a nestbox for this purpose.

Certain breeders position nestboxes as high as possible, in the belief that

Hollowed logs for parrot nesting most closely duplicate the sites preferred by most species in the wild.

Nests made of metal cans are attractive to parrot keepers because of their durability and ease of cleaning; however, they can be problematical with respect to temperature and humidity.

the birds commonly lay in tree hollows great distances from the ground. This is true in many cases, but conversely, successful breedings of macaws of the forest canopies have taken place in open-topped boxes located on the aviary floor. The most significant factor appears to be whether the parrots feel secure in their quarters, especially their nestbox, irrespective of the height at which it is

Perhaps more than in other parrot genera, the *Ara* macaws are inclined to hybridize if housed together. Shown here are a Green-wing (*A. chloroptera*) and a Blue-and-Gold (*A. ararauna*).

Kegs adapt well to being used as parrot nests; however, they have recently become more difficult to obtain.

positioned.

Wooden nestboxes are widely used today, although parrots have nested in hollow logs and other containers. Coconut husks were popular during the early 1900s for smaller species, and here up to eight parrotlets have been reared in such surroundings. Nestboxes came into favor when budgerigars were being bred in large numbers during the 1920s, and many different designs have been used since then.

The general pattern of most nestboxes is similar, consisting simply of four sides with a roof and floor. The actual angle of the nestbox has been varied on occasions, with a view to permitting easier access, either for the parrots or their keeper. Today, rectangular designs are used almost universally.

Timber to form the sides of the nestbox should be at least 1 inch (2.5 cm) in thickness for the smaller species, and increased accordingly for larger parrots. Thick wood helps to insulate the interior of the box, and so improves the internal environment for the hatching and rearing of chicks. In addition, most parrots like to whittle away the woodwork of their box when spending long periods inside. They may gnaw their way right through thin wood, resulting in the loss of eggs and chicks. The majority seem to prefer nestboxes with relatively small interiors. The following table gives a guide to sizes of nestboxes for a range of parrots.

Many breeders provide a wire mesh or hard plastic ladder of some kind inside the nestbox, to help the parrots move back and forth. This must be fixed firmly and safely in position, with no loose ends of wire remaining accessible to the parrots.

**Facing page:** A Senegal Parrot (*Poicephalus senegalus*) perched atop a keg nest.

## TABLE OF NESTBOX SIZES

| Species | Nestbox Height | Breadth | Width |
|---|---|---|---|
| Lovebirds | 9 in (23 cm) | 8 in (20 cm) | 6 in (15 cm) |
| *Poicephalus* Parrots | 12 in (30 cm) | 10 in (25 cm) | 10 in (25 cm) |
| Lories, *Pionus* Parrots | 20 in (50 cm) | 10 in (25 cm) | 10 in (25 cm) |
| Amazons, Grey Parrot | 20 in (50 cm) | 12 in (30 cm) | 12 in (30 cm) |
| Smaller Cockatoos | 20 in (50 cm) | 12 in (30 cm) | 12 in (30 cm) |
| Large Cockatoos | 20 in (50 cm) | 18 in (45 cm) | 18 in (45 cm) |
| Large Macaws | 36 in (90 cm) | 30 in (75 cm) | 30 in (75 cm) |

(These are intended as a guide, and need not be interpreted rigorously.)

There is otherwise a risk that the ladder could become loose. If it falls down, then it will block off the bottom. Netting staples provide probably the most secure means of fixing a ladder in place.

The amount of light entering the nestbox is important, since if the interior is well-lit, it may be ignored by the parrots. Most nestboxes are supplied with round entrance holes, presumably to simulate the appearance of natural tree hollows, but it is easier and equally satisfactory to cut a square entrance. This should be near the roof of the structure.

A further advantage of a square entry hole is that the parrots themselves will have easier access, since they can grip the sides more effectively. A piece of dowelling or a branch should be fitted just below the entrance, so the parrots do not have to fly directly onto the entry hole.

The roof section can be hinged for inspection purposes, although it may be difficult to look inside once the box is hung up in the aviary. You can also include a separate inspection flap on the side, well above the base so that the cut edges should be out of reach of the parrots within. Use

**Facing page:** If the aviary is spacious enough, pairs in mixed collections will proceed to breed. The parrots accommodated here include a Scarlet Macaw (*Ara macao*) and a Sulphur-crested Cockatoo (*Cacatua galerita*).

screws to assemble the nestbox if possible. This will ensure that it can be dismantled without difficulty, and damaged sections are easily replaced.

In the days when the brewing industry was more dependent on wooden casks rather than metal barrels for transporting beer, these solid containers, which were reinforced with metal supports, proved ideal for breeding macaws and cockatoos. You may be able to find such casks today, but if not, then strengthening of a solidly-constructed nestbox for such species will be essential.

You can nail sheeting over all the exposed edges of woodwork, including the entrance hole. Take care to ensure that the sheeting is carefully folded wherever possible, so the parrots will not cut their feet on sharp edges of the metal. Modified dustbins are far less satisfactory as nesting sites for these larger parrots, partly because they become very hot inside. In addition, the birds are unable to gnaw, and condensation may favor the spread of molds as well as poor hatchability.

The floor covering of the nestbox is important. Damp peat has been used, but this dries out and then becomes very dusty. Far

**Facing page:** A Thick-billed Parrot (*Rhynchopsitta pachyrhyncha*) perched in front of an artificial nesting log.

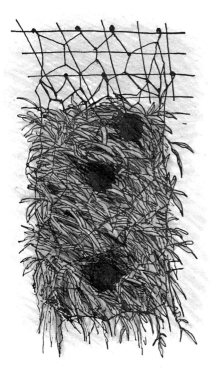

**Above:** A bale of twigs can be installed near the aviary roof, in which the birds will make nest holes.

**Facing page:** The only parrot species that constructs a nest of twigs in the fashion of so many other birds is the Monk, or Quaker, Parakeet (*Myiopsitta monachus*), seen here at its nest hole.

more satisfactory is the provision of short lengths of softwood in the interior of the nestbox which the parrots can gnaw to create a lining.

The vast majority of parrots do not actually build a nest, with the notable exception of the lovebirds and hanging parrots. They will strip off bark and leaves from branches, carrying these to the nestbox. The actual type of nest depends upon the species. Fischer's Lovebirds, for example, build a relatively domed structure, whereas Abyssinians prepare just a simple pad, usually of their own feathers, for the eggs.

Since the nestboxes are quite heavy structures in many cases, you will need to ensure that they are

firmly fixed in position in the aviary. Brackets can be used to secure the box to a vertical support, or a supporting platform may be required if a barrel is being provided.

## BREEDING BEHAVIOR

There is no fixed breeding season for parrots, although certainly once settled in their quarters, the majority tend to nest during the warmer months of the year. The Madagascar Lovebird is a notable exception however, and for this reason, pairs are best wintered indoors, with a nestbox available. As parrots should be supplied with a nestbox throughout the year for roosting purposes, eggs are occasionally produced outside this period. This is especially likely with the more free-breeding species such as the Peach-faced Lovebird, so nesting material should be withheld when these parrots are not required to breed.

Senegals and other *Poicephalus* parrots also sometimes lay during the winter months. Under these circumstances, you may want to leave the hen to incubate, and then consider removing any chicks, should the weather be cold. If you suspect that a hen is laying at this time of year,

**Facing page:** A Peach-faced Lovebird (*Agapornis roseicollis*) atop one of the proportionately tall nest boxes many lovebird breeders favor.

keep a close watch to ensure that she does not become egg-bound.

When breeding, parrots usually become more destructive, attacking any accessible woodwork in their aviary. Larger parrots, such as Amazons and cockatoos, may actively turn against their owners and occasionally bite without provocation, especially close to their nest site. The pair bond is frequently strengthened by mutual feeding and preening at this time, and the birds are likely to be more noisy.

On occasions, you may notice that the parrot's eyes become more colorful for a short period.

A pair of Golden-capped Conures (*Aratinga auricapilla*) beside their nest box, conventional in design.

This is caused by a constriction of the pupils, usually indicative of sexual excitement. It may be linked with body movements, such as head bobbing.

Only one mating is required to fertilize the whole clutch of eggs. Most Central and South

**Facing page:** At nine weeks of age, a young Blue-crowned Conure (*Aratinga acuticaudata*) is ready to begin to eat on its own.

**Below:** At four weeks of age, the feathers of these *Pionus* hybrid chicks (*P. menstruus x P. senilis*) are just beginning to unfurl.

Wooden nest boxes, such as the one containing this Yellow-headed Amazon (*Amazona ochrocephala*), allow the parrots to shape the entrance to their liking, as they would be required to do in the wild.

American parrots mate with the cock bird keeping one foot on the perch, and gripping his mate with the other. In other cases, the male may balance entirely on the female's back.

But mating in the case of cockatoos is not necessarily a sign that egg-laying is imminent. Compatible pairs may mate throughout the year, without nesting for much of this period. Keep a watch on pairs, as on occasion, aggression can develop, with a cock driving a hen if she refuses to mate. Serious assaults are most likely to arise again with cockatoos. It may be necessary to separate the birds, to prevent a fatal outcome.

Incubation rarely starts

immediately after the first egg is laid. In most species, the hen sits alone, although the cock will feed her, and often roosts alongside her in the nestbox at night. Male cockatoos are a noted exception however, since in the case of most species, they share the incubation duties with their partners, sitting alone for much of the day.

There is no need to disturb the parrots during the incubation period, unless there is a reason to suspect that all may not be going well. Some larger parrots can prove actively hostile. A close watch on the amount of food consumed will provide an early indication of possible trouble. Later this will also serve as a guide to the presence of chicks, which may be heard calling at intervals from within the nestbox.

Sun Conure, *Aratinga solstitialis*, with an egg she laid.

Most pairs may tolerate a mild degree of interference, but it is unwise to attempt an inspection of the nest while the hen is still in the box. Apart from the risk of any unhatched eggs being broken, chicks may also be injured or even killed by a frantic hen who has been disturbed. Actual desertion of the nest is not common in the case of parrots, but the presence of animals such as mice, or lights being flashed around the nestbox, drawing the hen out, can have this effect.

Many parrots emerge from the nestbox for a brief time at feeding time. This is probably the most suitable moment to inspect the nest quietly, while the birds are distracted by food.

Various items, such as soaked seeds will be invaluable for rearing purposes through the breeding period.

Once the young parrots have fledged, they will still return to roost in the nestbox at night. During these early days, they are fed largely by the cock, until they are eating independently. At this stage, it is advisable to remove the youngsters, in case their parents start to attack them. They may even be fatally injured, especially in the case of more prolific species, such as lovebirds and parrotlets. The adult birds resent the close proximity of their earlier young, and so attempt to drive them away, but are restricted by the confines of their enclosure.

A pair of Jandaya Conures, *Aratinga jandaya*, at the entrance of a nesting log.

If you are breeding parrots on a colony system, housing more than one pair in an aviary, then outbreaks of fighting at some stage are almost certain to arise. It is for this reason that pairs are usually housed individually.

**BREEDING PROBLEMS**

Provided that you have started with a true pair of parrots, they should make an attempt to nest, assuming they are being housed in suitable surroundings, and properly fed. But you may need to be patient.

Imported parrots can take three years or so before they attempt to breed, while hand-raised youngsters are unlikely to be mature before this age. This applies to the larger species, such as Amazons, macaws and cockatoos. Parrotlets, for example, will breed during their second year.

Eggs which fail to hatch may be infertile, and so appear relatively 'clear' when viewed in front of a light. Those which are opaque are likely to have contained an embryo which died in the shell. Such deaths can result from environmental factors such as chilling and low humidity, or possibly an inherited weakness. Mineral deficiencies may also be a cause of poor hatchability.

Should a hen die during the incubation period, the eggs can either be moved to an incubator, or transferred to another pair. The foster parents should ideally have laid about the same time as the original pair, so the chicks should be of a similar age when they hatch. Cock birds will not incubate eggs, even if they lose their mates, and are likely to ignore any chicks. These will need to be raised by hand if they are to survive.

Plucking of young parrots in the nestbox can become a major problem, especially with some

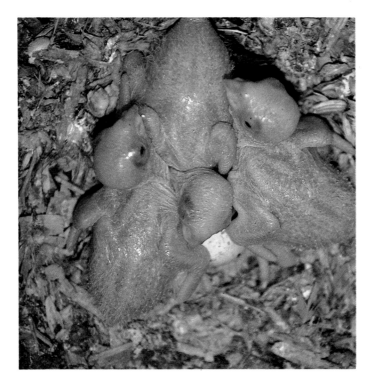

Canary-winged Parakeet (*Brotogeris versicolorus*) nestlings, two weeks old. At hatching, parrot chicks are naked or sparsely covered with down.

lories and lorikeets. Every round of chicks emerges plucked, with feathers being removed from the back of the neck and top of the wings in the first instance.

Feather-plucking is

most common in more prolific species, and may represent an attempt by the parent birds to persuade their youngsters to leave the nest, so they can lay again. The young birds themselves soon feather up, but until then, they are more susceptible to the effects of cold, being deprived of their natural insulation.

## HAND-RAISING

With incubators, it is now quite possible to rear parrot chicks by hand

The feathers emerge from the chick's skin covered by a sheath that soon disintegrates. This is a Canary-winged Parakeet.

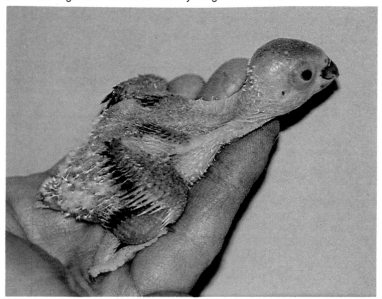

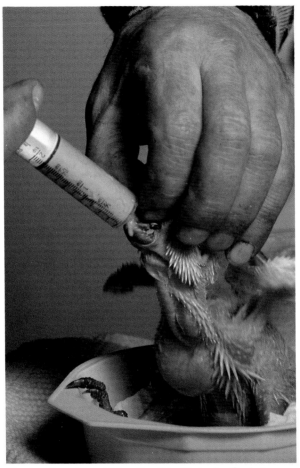

For hand-rearing, chicks, like this Umbrella Cockatoo
(*Cacatua alba*), can be fed with a syringe.

from hatching, but this obviously entails a considerable amount of work. If you are unable to do so yourself, you may be able to contact a parrot-rearing service in your area. Some parrots prove very poor parents, and if the chicks are to survive, they must be fed by hand.

Specially formulated foods for hand-raising parrot chicks are now available and help to overcome the nutritional problems which could otherwise be encountered. Follow the recommendations on the pack when mixing the food. You will also need a small spoon, with its edges bent to form a tube. This makes an ideal feeding implement, compared with a syringe, which is more likely to cause the young parrot to choke, as food has to be squirted into its mouth.

The chicks will need to be kept warm in a brooder, which can be a simple box heated by light-bulbs. Check the temperature with a thermometer close to where the birds are positioned. At first, for newly-hatched chicks, this needs to be close to the incubator temperature of 37.5 degrees C (99.5 degrees F). It can then be gradually reduced.

If the chicks are too hot, they will spread out as far as possible from each other, with their mouths open. They will need to be restrained from moving too far around the brooder in any event by placing them in a small cardboard box or similar

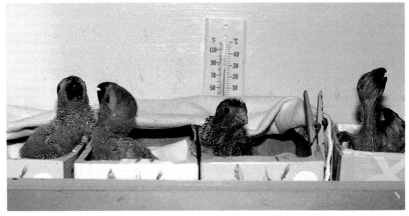

A brooder is used to house these Grey (and one Superb) parrot chicks that are being hand-raised.

open-topped container lined with kitchen towelling. Change this bedding at each feed.

The first few days will be critical, but once the chicks are used to the routine, they usually feed greedily. Wipe off any food which sticks to their soft beaks, since this is likely to harden and cause subsequent malformation. Between feeds, the crop where food is stored, located at the top of the chest, should slacken as the mixture passes through the digestive tract. If it fails to empty, this is a potentially serious problem, but it may be corrected by a gentle massage, and the administration of a solution of molasses and water.

Weigh the chicks each day, so that you can keep a check on their development. Just before they would normally leave the nest, they may become rather restless, and reluctant to feed. This is not necessarily a cause for concern, with slight weight loss being normal at this stage.

Breeder cages are recommended for chicks once they have feathered, and these should include a low perch. Gradually, the young parrots will have to be weaned onto a more solid diet. You can start adding ground-up sunflower seed kernels during the rearing period, and then the chicks will start taking increasing amounts once they are becoming independent.

At this point, those which are likely to be kept for breeding purposes, rather than as pets, should be introduced to others of their own kind, preferably of a similar age. This is particularly important if they have been reared on their own, so they do not become imprinted with a human identity. But remember that although captive-bred, such youngsters will not be hardy. They should be transferred to outside flights only when the weather is favorable.

# *Parrots as Pets*

Pet parrots bring an immeasurable amount of pleasure to millions of people all over the world, ranging from tribespeople in the Amazon basin and parts of Africa to the occupants of high-rise blocks in large cities. All appreciate the personality and mimicry for which parrots are famous. There are few pets more suitable for house-bound people, as tame parrots require a considerable amount of time devoted to them each day, if they are not to become bored.

Choose a species which is most suited to your own requirements, since they differ significantly in terms of behavior and needs. Amazons, for example, tend to have harsher calls than Greys, and although this aspect may not worry you, it could upset a close neighbor. All parrots can use their beaks effectively. Those of the larger macaws and cockatoos are especially powerful, making them more difficult for the novice owner to handle effectively.

The temperaments of Amazons and cockatoos can change for periods, once they are mature and in breeding condition. This can be particularly significant for the pet owner, unless he is aware of this change. The birds may also become more noisy and destructive as well at this stage.

The cost of a purchase is increasingly significant, since bigger parrots are invariably more expensive than their smaller relatives. This may obviously influence your choice. Whatever species attracts you, however, try to obtain a hand-raised youngster, even though this will be relatively costly.

The enjoyment of having a truly tame pet from the onset will be more than adequate compensation over the years ahead. Bearing in mind that the parrot should be part of your family for several decades, it is much better to wait a few months or so to obtain the ideal pet,

rather than gambling on one which may never settle properly with you.

A graphic account of what can then happen under these circumstances was written by C. W. Gedney back in 1879. The Green-winged Macaw involved proved to be completely untameable, in spite of every attempt made by its owner to win the bird's confidence. It was such a problem in the house that it was finally banished to the stables with a bull terrier dog as a companion.

Shortly afterwards, there was a bloody battle between the two, which left the terrier dead and the macaw virtually featherless with two broken wings. Its horrified owner hoped that its injuries would

A hand-tame parrot, such as this Yellow-headed Amazon (*Amazona ochrocephala*) will afford its owner considerable entertainment.

make the parrot more approachable, and so it was not destroyed. The macaw was nursed back to health, but the bird remained so aggressive that, very sadly, it was ultimately poisoned.

Yet if you obtain a young, hand-raised bird of this species, there are few more gentle companions in the avian world, irrespective of their powerful beaks. Usually the eyes provide a useful means of recognizing a young parrot, should you be in any doubt. The other option which you may want to consider is to choose an established tame and talking parrot. This generally proves more expensive, unless the bird is providing a problem for its present owner for one reason or another: perhaps it is very noisy.

Remember that adult tame parrots should have formed a strong bond with their previous owner. They will not necessarily take to you as readily as will a young parrot. They may even have acquired a mistrust or even dislike for people of one sex. Such behavior can usually be traced back to a previous instinct in their past history, but such upsets are not easily reversed.

## POINTERS ABOUT PET PARROTS

Lovebirds are popular as pets in Australia, but elsewhere, they are not widely kept for this purpose. They will prove personable pets however, and are now available in a wide range of colors, at relatively low cost. The Peach-faced probably settles best in the home, tending to be slightly bolder by nature than related species. They can be taught a few words, but are not talented talkers.

Parrotlets, in contrast,

are far less likely to prove tame and talk, unless you start with a hand-raised youngster. In addition, they can prove highly aggressive towards each other if they are confined in a limited space. The diet of hanging parrots usually renders them unsuitable for the domestic environment. They will often defecate through the bars of their

Parrots employ their beaks for moving about, so it's usual for them to test a finger before climbing onto it, as this Peach-fronted Conure (*Aratinga aurea*) is doing—a Cockatiel looks on.

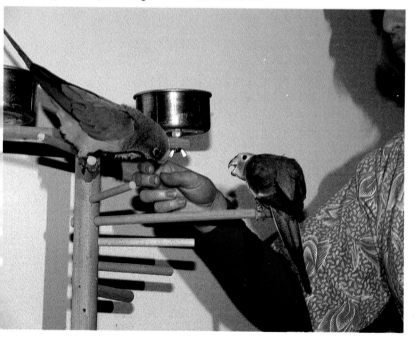

cage, over surrounding
furniture as they climb
around or roost here.

While hanging parrots
do not usually talk, lories
and lorikeets can prove

In view of their potential as pets,
the eight species of *Pionus* parrots
deserve to be better known. This is
the Dusky Parrot, *Pionus fuscus*.

good mimics. But again, their diet makes them unsuitable as indoor companions for many people.

Although the Grey Parrot is accepted as the best talking species, these birds can be shy and reluctant to display their talents in front of strangers. They are also rather sensitive by nature, and prone to the vice of feather-plucking. But few parrots make better companions, once they are settled in the home.

The small African *Poicephalus* parrots are less well-known as pets than the Grey, and considerably cheaper. These medium-sized birds are not noisy. Their calls consist of a series of rasping whistles, and they can be taught a few words, although they will never acquire the vocabulary of a Grey Parrot. If you obtain a genuine youngster, preferably reared by hand, then you can be assured of a devoted and easily-managed pet. As with other parrots, adults will not settle well in the home, and always remain nervous.

Various species of Amazon parrot are kept as pets. They may vary somewhat in their talking abilities, with the small White-fronted Amazon reputed to be less talented in this regard than other species such as the Blue-fronted Amazon. The *Pionus* parrots also originate from Central and South America, and although seen less often than Amazons, youngsters make delightful pets. The Blue-headed is probably more attractive than Maximilian's Parrot, but both are quiet and will talk if given proper training. A further point in their favor is that they are usually less expensive than either Amazons or Grey Parrots.

In the case of the macaws, the larger species are most eye-catching, with their multi-colored plumage, but can prove rather big for some homes. The smaller, dwarf macaws are frequently easier for the average person to handle and house satisfactorily. But whichever type of macaw is chosen, you should be certain of having an affectionate pet. These parrots usually become very attached to their owners. They may also learn several words or phrases.

Cockatoos are invariably very lively birds, and active by nature. As with other parrots, they really need spacious surroundings in the home, so purchase an indoor flight rather than a small cage. Kept in these surroundings, and given proper attention, cockatoos are then far less likely to pluck their feathers.

## SETTLING IN

Before you leave to collect your new pet, try to make all necessary preparations beforehand. Have the flight cage ready, and then after providing fresh water, you will simply need to transfer the parrot into its new home. Even a tame parrot may take a few days to settle down. At first, leave the bird quietly on its own, with its food and water provided within easy reach. Near a perch is ideal, as the parrot may hesitate to feed from the floor. Check that the bird has eaten later in the day, and that its droppings appear normal.

Moluccan Cockatoo, *Cacatua moluccensis.*

You must ensure that the cage is located out of drafts and direct sunlight, which could prove fatal. Avoid kitchens, or other parts of your home where there are fumes, since birds can die very rapidly when exposed to small volumes of poisonous gases. A room which is kept at a relatively constant temperature is to be preferred. You can buy a stand for most cages or, alternatively, use a firm table as a base unit. This will ensure that the cage cannot be knocked over accidentally. The ideal height, to let you have easy contact with your bird, is just below eye-level.

If you have acquired a

young, hand-raised parrot, then the bird is already likely to be finger-tame. It will sit on your hand without any concern, and can be rewarded with a piece of fruit. But if you need to train the parrot yourself, this is likely to prove a far more protracted process.

Start by persuading your new pet to perch on your gloved hand, while it is still within the cage. Always move slowly, so as to avoid upsetting the parrot. You can encourage the bird by starting with your hand close to the perch, and raising it up over the top. Then the parrot should step from the perch onto the hand, and remain there.

The next step is to slide your hand slowly from the cage, with the parrot remaining in place here. The length of time taken to reach this stage is variable, depending to some extent as to how long you can spend with your parrot. Some will tame much quicker than others. You should ideally set aside periods of time each day for training purposes, lasting perhaps ten minutes or so. At the end of each period, the parrot should be given a reward in the form of a piece of fruit or a similar item, which it is encouraged to take from the hand. It is surprising how gentle the larger parrots can be, in spite of their large beaks.

Once your parrot is tame enough to come out of its cage regularly, you must still always keep it supervised. Otherwise it could harm itself in the room, quite apart from damaging furniture. Avoid plants which are poisonous, and always close and screen the windows so there will be no risk of the bird escaping or injuring itself.

Many tame parrots are content to spend most of their time either with their owner, or perched on top of their flight cage. You can also obtain special 'T'-shaped stands, with a tray for droppings beneath. If you have one of these, do not be tempted to chain your parrot to it. If the bird becomes frightened by the presence of a cat in the room, for example, it may try to fly off, injuring itself badly because of the restraining chain.

You will need to be particularly careful if introducing a new parrot to an established pet. Never try to place the newcomer directly into a confrontation situation, but allow the birds to become acquainted on neutral territory, out of their cages. It is unwise to leave one parrot free in the room, while the other remains confined. Either or both could then end up with a bitten and bleeding foot, as they are free to climb around the single cage.

Larger parrots can also become jealous of other pets such as dogs. They will not hesitate to show their dislike by screeching loudly, or even nipping the unfortunate animal if they have the opportunity. Try to avoid having this situation arise by making a fuss of the parrot at the same time as attention is being lavished on the dog, so the bird does not feel ignored.

## TALKING PARROTS

Some species are more talented talkers than others, and individuals also vary in their powers of mimicry. You will need both patience and an interested pupil if the parrot is to learn to talk well. Start by ensuring there are no other distractions in the room, such as other members of the family moving about. Regular short lessons will give the best results. Repeat the chosen phrase at every opportunity until the bird has mastered the sound. You may be able to purchase pre-recorded cassette tapes to help with training, but these will feature an unfamiliar voice, and will not hold the bird's attention as well as a person in the room.

Once your parrot starts to speak, you can slowly expand its vocabulary. But do not try to rush your pet at this stage, otherwise its speech is likely to become muddled, with phrases and words jumbled as a result. The end result may be truly spectacular. Grey parrots in particular can build up impressive vocabularies, which may exceed 800 words.

One of the most valuable phrases to teach a parrot is an address or telephone number, just in case it ever escapes. This simple lesson has helped to reunite a number of owners with their pets.

# *Ailments*

The exotic appearance of many parrots may suggest that they are perhaps somewhat delicate and prone to illness. While a few rare species, such as the pygmy parrots *(Micropsitta),* have indeed proved hard to maintain, the vast majority are easy to care for, and long-lived, provided that they are kept in clean surroundings and fed well.

Always keep a close watch on newly-acquired birds, especially if they have been imported. The stress of movement and unfamiliar surroundings will have lowered the parrot's resistance to disease. In addition, it may well encounter unfamiliar harmful micro-organisms in its new environment, to which established stock on the premises is virtually immune.

## SIGNS OF ILLNESS

A sick parrot usually appears fluffed up and sits with both feet on the perch when sleeping, rather than altering its grip as is normal (except often in young birds). It will appear dull, and reluctant to move unless approached closely. Its appetite is often reduced, perhaps to the extent of refusing all food, while the droppings may have changed in color and consistency. The eyes are often closed for long periods, and the wings droop, sometimes being held slightly away from the body.

The condition of a parrot showing signs of lethargy will rapidly deteriorate, unless immediate action is taken. In severe cases, you may just find the bird on the floor of the cage or flight in obvious distress. But with more chronic afflictions, these signs will be less apparent, at least in the early stages.

There may just be a loss of vitality, with a closer examination revealing that the parrot is "going light." This loss of weight is easily detected by being able to feel either side of the breastbone quite distinctly, as a sharp prominence. In a healthy bird, this area is covered by muscle tissue.

Actual diagnosis of the conditions afflicting parrots is far less straightforward, because symptoms tend to be generalized in most cases. Seek the advice of an experienced avian veterinarian as soon as possible therefore, having transferred the bird to a warm environment. You can purchase hospital cages suitable for the smaller parrots.

Alternatively, an infra-red lamp can be used as a heat source, simply suspended over the parrot's cage. Choose one of the dull-emitter type, which gives out heat rather than light, so the parrot is not kept under the glare of a bright light. You can include a separate low wattage light bulb, to give the parrot more time to feed, but periods of darkness are necessary.

A heat controller of some kind connected to the infra-red lamp will enable you to regulate the output, with the light itself being switched on as darkness falls. You can then switch this off around midnight, ensuring that the infra-red heater will keep the parrot warm around the clock.

Avoid handling a sick or injured parrot more than is absolutely necessary, because subjecting it to this additional stress may well prove fatal. This applies especially to birds which are not used to being handled. Always take sensible precautions yourself, to prevent spread of disease, either to other birds or even yourself. Wash your hands thoroughly after having dealt with sick parrots, and attend to their needs after those of healthy stock. Sick parrots should always be isolated until it is certain they have fully recovered.

## ANTIBIOTIC TREATMENT

Antibiotics have proved to be a major help to the bird-keeper in counteracting disease but as with all remedies, they must be used strictly in accordance with the dosage instructions stated on the container. Since they act by disrupting bacterial development, antibiotics will affect both beneficial as well as harmful bacteria, especially if given in excess. This in turn makes it easier for other damaging micro-organisms to establish themselves in the body, once its natural defenses have been breached.

Fungal infections, for example, can often be linked directly to improper use of antibiotics. Other side-effects, such as vitamin deficiencies, can also result.

Often, you will find that a parrot shows a very rapid recovery once antibiotic treatment begins. But always use the medication as directed, and do not be tempted to cut the course short as a result.

Otherwise, this gives bacteria an opportunity to develop resistance to the drug, which may make it ineffective in the future.

In some areas, you can purchase antibiotic treatments for birds from your pet stores, whereas in Britain, you will need to obtain them from a veterinarian. For smaller parrots, such as lovebirds, there is special seed available, which has been impregnated with antibiotics. Powdered preparations, to be mixed in the drinking water, offer another means of treatment, which may be used in conjunction with medicated seed.

For larger species such as macaws, it is sometimes possible to give tablets, although this usually requires two people—one to hold the bird and keep its beak

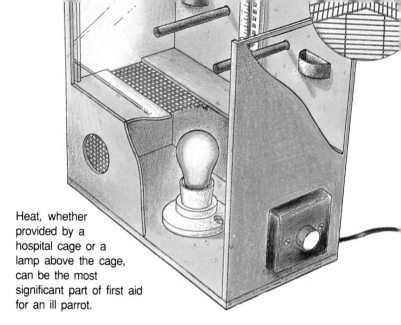

Heat, whether provided by a hospital cage or a lamp above the cage, can be the most significant part of first aid for an ill parrot.

open, while the other concentrates on dropping the tablet as far back in the mouth as possible. Closing the macaw's beak for a few moments will then encourage it to swallow the tablet, rather than having an opportunity to spit it out.

Although tablets can be very effective, guaranteeing the dosage of drug, the handling of the bird for this purpose is stressful. In an emergency situation, a veterinarian may opt for an injection, which can be given more easily.

For more serious problems consult a veterinarian, your bird store owner or a book on bird diseases.

# Species

The following pages cover a wide selection of the parrots which are popular pet and aviary birds. They are listed in groups, to help you decide which is most suited to your requirements. Then, for further information, you can consult some of the other titles in the wide range produced by T.F.H. Publications. Ask at your pet store for full details.

**Celestial Parrotlet—**
*Forpus coelestis*
Western Ecuador to northwest Peru.

Mainly green. Cocks have a bluish streak behind the eye, and a blue rump, whereas hens are green. Young birds are similar to adults.

These small members of the parrot family, averaging about 5 inches (12.5 cm) in length, are an ideal choice where space is limited. All five species in the genus *Forpus* can be sexed visually, and pairs will normally nest quite readily.

Although prolific, Celestial Parrotlets can be aggressive, especially when kept in cages. Some pairs may attack their chicks even before they fledge. If you see signs of aggression, you will need to remove the youngsters without delay. In any event, transfer them to separate accommodation as soon as you are sure that they are feeding independently. The adults are then likely to nest again.

Clutches numbering six eggs are not unusual. Incubation lasts about 18 days, and the chicks normally fledge when they are just under six weeks old. Although they are mature six months later, do not encourage them to breed until they are a year old.

## Green-rumped Parrotlet—*Forpus passerinus*

Northern South America, from Colombia to Brazil.

Predominantly yellowish-green, with dark blue wing coverts in the case of the cock. Hens have a yellowish forehead and brown legs. Youngsters have pinkish beaks.

A number of different forms of this parrotlet are recognized, but they are similar in terms of care. One pair per aviary is always to be recommended. Parrotlets will use commercially-available budgerigar nestboxes, and have a long reproductive life. A cock known to be at least eighteen years old has successfully sired chicks in Sweden. If you obtain imported stock, it is advisable to bring the birds indoors for their first winter, but after this, they should prove reasonably hardy.

## LOVEBIRDS

This group of nine species, found in Africa and on some offshore islands, has long been very popular in aviculture. Their

Green-rumped Parrot, *Forpus passerinus.*

experienced breeder however, while the Swindern's Black-collared Lovebird *(A. swinderniana)* is almost totally unknown in aviculture.

Out of the remainder,

Madagascar Lovebird, *Agapornis cana*, a male.

requirements are similar to those of parrotlets, and they are equally suitable for breeders with limited space at their disposal. The Red-faced Lovebird *(Agapornis pullaria)* is a species which can only be recommended to the

Celestial Parrotlets, *Forpus coelestis.*

the Madagascar Lovebird *(A. cana)* can be easily sexed, since only cocks have gray heads, as can the Abyssinian *(A. taranta),* with males only having a band of red plumage on their foreheads. The Madagascar proves a rather nervous species, and often tends to nest during the winter months. Neither species is well-established in aviculture, but if you can obtain stock, there is no reason why you should not be able to establish your own strain, with patience.

In the past, both Nyasa *(A. lilianae)* and Black-cheeked Lovebirds *(A. nigrigenis)* proved prolific in some collections, but have faded from the avicultural scene in recent years. The three species of lovebird which you are most likely to encounter today are as follows:

**Peach-faced Lovebird—**
*Agapornis roseicollis*
Southwest Africa.

Pinkish facial plumage, extending down to the throat, with the back of the head being green. Plumage of the underparts is lighter, while the rump is blue. Sexes are identical in appearance. Young birds have black markings on their beaks, and are duller.

This is undoubtedly the most widely-kept species of lovebird, and especially from the 1970s onward, a whole host of color forms have been bred, which has greatly enhanced its popularity. Among the colors are pastel blue (greenish-blue), lutino (bright yellow), and olive forms.

Peach-faced Lovebirds are hardy and easy to care for, but encourage them to roost under cover at night, otherwise they may suffer from frost bite. Although usually aggressive, it is possible to keep them successfully in small colonies, if you introduce the whole group to the aviary at the same time. By this means, pairs will then be formed, and if necessary, you can then move them to separate accommodation for breeding purposes.

Hens alone usually carry nesting material tucked in between the feathers of the back and rump, using it to build a cup-shaped hollow in the nestbox. The chicks hatch after a period of 23 days' incubation (as with other lovebird species), and are covered initially with thick red downy feathering. They fledge about six weeks later.

## Masked Lovebird—
## *Agapornis personata*

Northeastern Tanzania.

Blackish heads, yellow breasts, becoming green on the lower abdomen. Wings also green. Young birds, as in other cases, often have blackish markings on their beaks and are duller in coloration.

These lovebirds, slightly smaller than the Peach-faced, measure about 5.5 inches (14 cm) long. Again, it is impossible to sex pairs by sight. Hens use longer strips of nesting material, carrying it in their beaks in this instance. They construct a relatively domed nest, and it can be difficult to inspect the interior. Five eggs appear to form the average clutch, and pairs may nest twice in a season.

Color mutations in this species are less common, but there is a blue form, in which yellow plumage is replaced by white, while green areas are blue. Head coloration is unaffected. A yellowish form is also known, and when combined with the blue, has given rise to the white color form. This is simply a dilution of the color of the blue however, rather than a pure white.

## Fischer's Lovebird—
## *Agapornis fischeri*

Northwest Tanzania.

Bright red-orange head, predominantly green body and blue rump.

A close relative of the

Fischer's Lovebird, *Agapornis fischeri.*

previous species, Fischer's Lovebirds are still imported quite regularly. They must be acclimatized properly before being expected to overwinter in unheated outdoor accommodation. When breeding, some pairs prove persistently bad feather-pluckers, but providing chicks are not allowed to become chilled after fledging, they should

Black-cheeked Lovebird, *Agapornis nigrigenis.*

**Senegal Parrot— *Poicephalus senegalus***

Senegal and neighboring countries south of the Sahara.

Grayish-black head, green chest and wings, orangish-yellow belly. Young birds have dark eyes, whereas those of adults have bright yellow irises.

The *Poicephalus* Parrots form a group of eight parrots, also originating from Africa. They have tended to be rather neglected in aviculture, but offer considerable scope for those who wish to specialize in a particular genus.

regrow their feathers quite rapidly. Again, this is not a species which can be sexed visually, but its calls are likely to be less disturbing to near neighbors than those of the Peach-faced.

The Senegal Parrot is the best-known member of the genus in birdkeeping circles. Adults can be shy at first, but usually settle well in aviary surroundings and prove hardy once acclimatized properly. Unfortunately it is not possible to sex them by visual means. Hens will often flare their tails like lovebirds near their nestbox, when they are in breeding condition. Measuring just 9 inches (22.5 cm) long, this is one of the smaller species, but can still prove destructive towards any exposed woodwork in their quarters.

**Meyer's Parrot—**
*Poicephalus meyeri*
Southern Central Africa.

Brownish head, back and wings with bluish-green underparts. Variable areas of yellow coloration, especially on the crown of the head and at the shoulders. Youngsters have brown irises, whereas those of adults are orangish-red.

Similar in size to the Senegal Parrot, members of this species can show noticeable variations in coloration. But these are not indicative of sexual dimorphism, but rather of subspecific differences, between birds from different parts of their range.

As with other *Poicephalus* parrots, Meyer's appear to prefer a nestbox located in a reasonably dark position in their aviary. Three or four eggs are laid, with the incubation period lasting about 26 days. Youngsters usually leave the nest after 8 weeks or so. *Poicephalus* parrots outside the breeding season in groups, but pairs need individual accommodation when nesting.

**Grey Parrot—*Psittacus erithacus***

Across most of Central Africa.

Largely grey, apart from the tail and tail coverts which are scarlet. Whitish bare skin around the eyes. Irises are yellow in mature birds, and dark in youngsters.

The Grey Parrot is well-known as a pet, and now many more are also being bred annually in collections around the world. These parrots do vary in coloration through their range, and this affects their price. As a general rule, Timneh Grey Parrots, with their darker overall plumage and maroon tails are less costly than those with scarlet feathering. Timnehs originate from the western side of the species' range.

There are also paler Greys, sometimes described as "Silvers" which come from the Congo. These may be slightly larger than others occurring elsewhere. On average, Grey Parrots are about 14 inches (32.5 cm) in length.

These parrots cannot be sexed easily, although adult cocks can sometimes be recognized by their darker wings. Imported birds need

**Above:** Blue-crowned Hanging Parrot, *Loriculus galgulus.*

**Left:** Grey Parrot, *Psittacus erithacus.*

careful acclimatization, disliking cold, damp weather. It may take several years for them to settle in their quarters before starting to breed. Grey Parrots can live for fifty years or more.

Sumatra.

Mainly green, with blue on the crown of the head and a red rump. Hens lack the red throat markings of cocks, with reduced areas of blue on the head, and yellowish

Vernal Hanging Parrot, *Loriculus vernalis*.

### Blue-crowned Hanging Parrot—*Loriculus galgulus*

The Malay Peninsula, and neighboring islands, including Borneo and

plumage on the mantle. Youngsters are duller than hens.

The name of these interesting little parrots, averaging about 5 inches

(12.5 cm) in length, comes from their habit of sleeping upside down off a perch, hanging on by one foot while the other is rested. You will need to check their claws regularly, because if these are overgrown, the hanging parrot can easily become caught up in its quarters, and may be injured as a result. They are not always easy birds to establish, and must be offered a varied diet, including the smaller cereal seeds, fruit and nectar. They will also benefit from one of the dry lory diets which are now available.

Always provide nectar in a drinker however, rather than an open pot. Otherwise the birds may attempt to bathe in the sticky nectar, with catastrophic results. Water for bathing should be provided in a shallow container, and changed regularly.

**Vernal Hanging Parrot— *Loriculus vernalis***

From southwest India to the Malay Peninsula and Indochina.

Largely green, with a red beak and rump. Cocks can usually be recognized by the blue markings on their throat. Young birds have orange beaks.

Another member of this group of ten species which is usually available, the Vernal Hanging Parrot can also be kept quite satisfactorily in a planted aviary. They rarely destroy vegetation, and are quite social by nature, although when breeding, some individuals can become aggressive. Like lovebirds, they build a nest in a suitable box, with the hen often carrying material tucked in among the feathers of her rump. She sits alone, laying four or five eggs on average which should hatch after a period of 20 days. Chicks fledge at just over a month old, and are independent about two weeks later. Mealworms and egg-based canary rearing foods are usually popular items with the adults when they are feeding the chicks.

Two clutches of eggs may be laid in the course of a year. In view of their unusual roosting habits, it can be better to overwinter hanging parrots indoors, but their surroundings must be easy to clean, because of their fairly liquid droppings. An interesting group of parrots, especially suitable if you have limited outdoor space available.

## Rainbow Lorikeet— *Trichoglossus haematodus*

Parts of Indonesia, New Guinea and neighboring islands, as well as northern and eastern parts of Australia.

Green back and wings, reddish-blue chest markings, becoming greenish-yellow below. Head blackish-blue, with yellowish-green area on the nape of the neck. Young birds have dark beaks.

The coloration of these lorikeets is variable, with many different forms

**Above:** Rainbow Lorikeet, *Trichoglossus haematodus.*

**Right:** Chattering Lory, *Lorius garrulus.*

occurring over the various islands where they are found. They may also be described under different names, with the widely-kept Green-naped Lorikeet being a member of this species. Although they cannot be sexed visually, it is sometimes possible to house a small group together in an aviary, and even breed them on a colony system.

**Above:** Moluccan Red Lory, *Eos bornea*.

**Right:** Dusky Lory, *Pseudeos fuscata*.

Pairs usually nest readily, but some prove bad feather-pluckers. Remove the young as soon as they are independent, because they may otherwise be attacked by their parents, especially if the adults are nesting again.

Two or three eggs form the average clutch, with the incubation period lasting about 25 days. Fledging occurs approximately 9 weeks later. Rainbow Lorikeets make a good introduction to this group of birds, and their calls are not as loud as those of some other species.

### Chattering Lory—*Lorius garrulus*

Moluccas, Indonesia.

Scarlet, with green wings and thighs. Youngsters again have brownish beaks and irises.

Lories can be distinguished from lorikeets by the shape of their tail, which is short and square, rather than tapering to a point. This particular species is slightly larger than the Rainbow Lorikeet, averaging about 12 inches (30 cm) in length. It is also somewhat noisier, as its name implies. Surgical sexing or a similar method will be required to identify a true pair. Again, two eggs will be laid and should hatch after a period of 25 days. Young birds leave the nest at 11 weeks old. There is also a yellow-backed race of this species, which originates from the islands of Obi, Batjan and Morotai, and is quite common in aviculture.

### Moluccan Red Lory—*Eos bornea*

Moluccan islands, Indonesia.

Mainly red, with blue and purple markings on

the wings and black flight feathers. Youngsters have a bluish tinge to their abdominal plumage.

Another species which has proved prolific under aviary surroundings, the Red Lory, like the other species listed here, is hardy, once properly acclimatized. Unfortunately, these lories are also quite noisy birds. Breeding details are similar to those of the Chattering Lory.

As with other members of the group, Red Lories have specialized tongues, with small, brush-like papillae at their tips. These help to remove pollen grains from the flowers, compressing them so they can be swallowed. They may also help to obtain nectar, but this is usually quite liquid, and therefore easily swallowed, even in small quantities.

**Dusky Lory—***Pseudeos fuscata*

New Guinea and neighboring islands.

Is a variable combination of olive-brown, mixed with reddish-orange markings. Some birds have yellow rather than orange markings. Hens often (but not always) have silvery-white rumps, whereas those of cocks are yellowish. Young birds have brown irises.

This was a rare species in aviculture until the middle of the 1970s. Since then, it has been bred on many occasions in collections around the world. Incubation lasts 24 days, with the chicks

leaving the nest for the first time when they are around 10 weeks old.

**Eclectus Parrot—*Eclectus roratus***

Moluccas, Solomon Islands, New Guinea and neighboring islands, and the Cape York Peninsula of Australia.

The most extreme example of sexual dimorphism of all parrots. Cocks are predominantly green, whereas hens are mainly red, with a dull purple abdomen. Young birds have dark brown rather than orangish irises.

These parrots, although relatively costly, are easy to look after, and breed quite readily.

**Facing page:** Eclectus Parrots, *Eclectus roratus*—the contrast between the red female and the green male is the most striking case of sexual dimorphism in parrots.

**Below:** Blue-headed Parrot, *Pionus menstruus.*

Interestingly, their digestive tract is exceptionally long, which suggests greenfood, buds and shoots naturally form an important part of their diet. You should provide greenfood; every day if possible, as well as fruit. Carrots will also prove a valuable source of Vitamin A. When deprived of such foods, Eclectus are liable to develop candidiasis. They are quite large parrots, measuring about 14 inches (35 cm).

Some hens can be aggressive towards intended mates, and should be watched accordingly. Introductions need to be carried out carefully, and you should include several food pots around the aviary, in case the hen tries to monopolize one. When breeding, two eggs form the usual clutch, and will take around 28 days to hatch. Add a supplement to the rearing food if necessary, as young Eclectus can develop rickets, but do not exceed the recommended dose.

Youngsters fledge at about 11 weeks old, and are sexually mature by their third year. It is not unusual for some pairs to produce chicks predominantly of one sex, although the reason for this is unclear. Young Eclectus can be sexed by the age of one month, when the feathers of their mantle are becoming apparent.

**Black-headed Caique—**
*Pionites melanocephala*
Northern South

America.

Black upper head, yellow on the sides of the neck and throat, as well as the thighs, white chest and abdomen and green wings. Young birds have horn-colored rather than grayish beaks.

This species, and the very similar White-bellied Caique, are lively, small parrots, measuring about 9 inches (22.5 cm) long. They are not especially common in collections, but make attractive aviary occupants, in spite of their noisy and rather destructive natures. You must provide them with adequate branches for gnawing, otherwise their beaks will soon become overgrown. Walnuts are a favorite treat, and fruit should form a significant part of their diet.

Unfortunately, they cannot be visually sexed. If you obtain recently-imported stock, the birds must be kept indoors for their first winter, unless the weather is extremely mild.

Breeding is most likely to be successful in fairly dark surroundings. Up to three eggs may be anticipated, hatching after a period of 28 days. Young birds should leave the nest when they are about 10 weeks old. Caiques have been known to live for several decades, but can fight viciously if strange birds are introduced to each other without proper supervision. Releasing all birds into the enclosure at the same time should help to avert any initial disputes. Breeding pairs

**Above:** Black-headed Caiques, *Pionites melanocephala.*

**Facing page:** Red-faced Lovebirds, *Agapornis pullaria.*

need to be housed on their own.

**Maximilian's Parrot—**
*Pionus maximiliani*

Eastern parts of Brazil into northern Argentina.
Dark green, with an olive tinge to the plumage, with mauvish-blue chin and throat. Blue with red barring under

the tail. Youngsters have reddish foreheads.

These parrots, measuring about 11 inches (27.5 cm) in length, show to best effect in an outside aviary, where the rich hues in their plumage are most apparent in sunlight. They are reasonably quiet, and not especially destructive. As with other *Pionus* parrots, they delight in bathing, and those kept as pets should be sprayed regularly. Young birds can become very tame, and may be taught to speak quite well.

### Blue-headed Parrot— *Pionus menstruus*

Central America, from Costa Rica southward to Peru and Bolivia.

Cobalt-blue head, greenish body and red feathering often in the region of the throat and under the tail. Young birds have a greener head, and red on the forehead.

The *Pionus* parrots are not widely-kept, but their care is straightforward, and they are easier to manage than many larger Amazon Parrots. As with most New World species however, they cannot be sexed reliably by visual means. Differences in the plumage of this species may well result from its wide range. Breeding details are similar to those of the Maximilian's Parrot.

Two or three eggs form the usual clutch, and the incubation period lasts for 26 days. Chicks fledge around 10 weeks old. Do not be surprised if a hen remains in the nestbox for some weeks before laying. This is quite common behavior, especially if the pair have not nested before. Avoid unnecessary disturbance, because these can prove rather nervous parrots, and they may injure their youngsters as a result.

When purchasing *Pionus* parrots, pay particular attention to their breathing, since the fungal disease aspergillosis is not uncommon in members of this genus. Others that you may encounter occasionally, out of the nine recognized species, are the Bronze-winged *(P. chalcopterus)* and Dusky *(P. fuscus)* parrots.

### Blue-fronted Amazon—
*Amazona aestiva*

Northeastern Brazil, extending south to Paraguay and northern Argentina.

Mainly green, except for red markings on the wings and tail. Also characteristic area of blue, variable in extent above the nostrils, and surrounding area of yellow on the head. Young birds are duller with brown irises.

This species is one of the best-known of all parrots. Many are kept as pets, and learn to talk well. Recently, more emphasis has been placed on keeping these and other Amazons as breeding birds. They tend to have a fairly well-defined nesting period, especially when housed in outdoor aviaries. Most pairs lay not during the spring like some parrots,

**Left:** Blue-fronted Amazon, *Amazona aestiva.*

**Below:** Meyer's Parrot, *Poicephalus meyeri.*

Yellow-headed Amazons, *Amazona ochrocephala*.

White-fronted Amazon, *Amazona albifrons*.

but late in early summer.

As a result, only one round of chicks is normally reared in a season, unless the first clutch of eggs is removed soon after laying. As many as five eggs can be laid in a clutch, and incubation tends to last around 26 days. The young will leave the nest at about 8 weeks old, although it may be an additional three years before they themselves breed successfully. Their lifespan, at least in captivity, can be nearly a century.

## Orange-winged Amazon—*Amazona amazonica*

Northern South America, extending south to eastern Peru and southern Brazil.

Similar to the Blue-fronted Amazon, but can be distinguished by its smaller size, orange rather than red wing markings and a horn-colored rather than black beak. It measures about 12 inches (30 cm) overall, whereas the Blue-front can be 15 inches (45 cm) or so. Young birds again have dark beaks.

This species is another which is often available, and imported with some regularity. Carefully acclimatize such birds, and add a supplement which contains Vitamin A to their diet when they are first acquired, as they may be suffering from a slight deficiency of this vitamin. Breeding results are presently less commonly reported than with the Blue-front, but pairs will nest quite readily. Orange-winged Amazons have even bred successfully in a large cage in the home.

## Yellow-headed Amazon—*Amazona ochrocephala*

From Mexico south to the Amazon basin and eastern Peru.

Exceedingly variable, in terms of yellow coloration. Body predominantly green. Yellow may form just a small band on the head, or extend over the whole head, as in the Double Yellow-headed form.

Youngsters again recognizable by their brown irises.

Most taxonomists recognize nine different races of this Amazon, which is found over a wide area of both Central and South America. As with most Amazons, no sexual differences are apparent in this case, so do not be misled by plumage variations between individuals when seeking pairs. At the start of the breeding period, Amazons often become aggressive, and more noisy than usual. This can be a particular problem if you live in an urban area, because they will call at first light, and are likely to disturb the neighborhood. Constriction of the pupils, coupled with tail flaring, are other characteristic signs of breeding condition in these parrots.

**White-fronted Amazon— *Amazona albifrons***

Central America, from the Pacific coast of Mexico to western Costa Rica.

Largely green, with red plumage encircling the eyes. A white band immediately above the nostrils, and bluish feathering on the crown of the head. The edges of the wings are generally red in cocks, and green in hens. Young birds have a reduced area of red, confined to the front of the eyes, rather than encircling them.

The smallest member of this genus of 27 species, measuring just 10 inches (25 cm) long, the White-fronted Amazon can also

Of the large macaws, the Blue-and-Gold (*Ara ararauna*) is no doubt the most familiar in captivity.

be sexed visually. These two factors make these parrots more suitable for many breeders, especially since they are also somewhat less noisy than their larger counterparts.

Breeding has become quite commonplace during recent years.

Incubation lasts about 25 days, and the young birds leave the nest at just over 7 weeks old. Up to four eggs can form the average clutch.

**Blue and Gold Macaw— *Ara ararauna***

Found over much of

northern South America, and in Central America from Panama to Colombia.

Blue back and wings, yellowish-golden underparts, with black plumage under the chin. Large area of mainly bare white facial skin.

These macaws rank among the largest members of the parrot family, averaging around 34 inches (85 cm). They are even capable of blushing, with their bare facial skin turning pinkish when they become excited. Compatible pairs usually breed quite readily, but in the case of young birds nesting for the first time, losses among resulting chicks may be high. In most cases, the adults soon learn to feed their

Scarlet Macaws (*Ara macao*) at the entrance to a nesting keg.

offspring properly.

Two eggs form the normal clutch, although three may be laid occasionally. The incubation period lasts about 28 days, and the resulting chicks develop slowly. They are nearly fully feathered at 10 weeks old, and leave the nest about three weeks later.

These macaws are likely to prove very destructive, and housing them adequately is an expensive undertaking. They can also prove noisy on occasions, especially when in breeding condition. Other similarly large species are the Red and Green (Green-winged, *A. chloroptera*) and the Red and Yellow (Scarlet, *A. macao*) macaws.

**Yellow-naped Macaw—**
*Ara auricollis*

Brazil through Bolivia and Paraguay into northwestern Argentina.

Predominantly green, with distinctive yellow collar around the neck, blackish face and white bare facial skin. Young birds have gray rather than pinkish feet.

As with other macaws, these cannot be sexed with any degree of certainty by their appearance. They are much smaller than the preceding species, measuring about 16 inches (40 cm), and one of the so-called group of dwarf macaws, all of which are largely green in color.

Yellow-naped Macaws are attractive, hardy birds, which soon become tame.

When excited or annoyed, they reveal their loud voices, but at other times, they have a relatively quiet call. In a large aviary, two pairs may agree together, but it is safer to house them individually. Care must always be taken when introducing macaws together for the first time. Some develop an immediate dislike for an intended partner. Introducing them on neutral territory is always less likely to lead to a rejection.

The incubation period for Yellow-naped Macaws is about 25 days, and the youngsters will leave the nestbox at approximately 11 weeks old.

Although this species has only been available from the mid-1970s, it is already well-established in aviculture. Youngsters are likely to be mature by three years of age, at an earlier stage than the bigger macaws.

### Red-shouldered Macaw—*Ara nobilis*

Eastern Venezuela and the Guianas southward to southern Brazil.

Green, with a blue forehead and red feathering along the outer edge of the wings. Youngsters have very little feathering, and red at the edge of the wings is replaced by a small area of orange.

These so-called 'mini' macaws are just 13 inches (32.5 cm) long. They usually agree well when kept on the colony system, and can prove quite prolific. Unlike their

Chestnut-fronted Macaw, *Ara severa*.

Lesser Sulphur-crested Cockatoo, *Cacatua sulphurea*.

larger relatives, Red-shouldered or Hahn's Macaws can prove double-brooded, and lay clutches of up to five eggs.

Surprisingly, few are kept as pets, although one which lived in Vienna, Austria was reputed to have learned over 50 words. The hen incubates alone, with the chicks hatching after a period of 25 days. They should leave the nest at about 8 weeks old.

Swinderen's Black-collared Lovebird, *Agapornis swinderniana*.

**Lesser Sulphur-crested Cockatoo—*Cacatua sulphurea***

Sulawesi (formerly Celebes) and neighboring islands.

White, with pale lemon ear coverts and a bright yellow crest, except in the case of the subspecies known as the Citron-crested, where yellow coloration is replaced by orange. Hens can usually be distinguished by their reddish-brown irises, whereas those of cocks are black.

Six different forms of this cockatoo are recognized across the various islands where it occurs, of which the Citron-crested (described above) from the island of Sumba is most distinctive. The smallest form is the Timor race, which, at about 10 inches (25 cm) is about 3 inches (7.5 cm) less than the average size of these cockatoos.

Lesser Sulphur-crested Cockatoos have been bred quite frequently, although pairs often prove nervous when nesting. Take care when entering their aviary at this time, especially with tame birds, as they may not hesitate to attack you if you venture near the nestbox.

A major problem when breeding cockatoos is to persuade them to sample a suitable variety of rearing foods to sustain their chicks. Try to encourage them to feed on as wide a range of foods as possible, well before the start of the breeding season, so as to avoid this problem.

Two eggs form the usual clutch, and these should hatch after a period of about 25 days. Young birds are usually feeding themselves by 3 months old, and should be removed to separate accommodation without delay.

**Moluccan Cockatoo—**
*Cacatua moluccensis*
Islands of the South Moluccas, Indonesia.

Light salmon-pink coloration overall, with deep pinkish-red crest feathers. The crest in this case is broad, and curls back towards the neck. Cocks have black irises, whereas those of hens tend to be reddish-brown.

These large cockatoos, averaging around 25 inches (63.5 cm) in size make truly spectacular aviary occupants, but only if you have no close neighbors who would object to their loud, far-carrying calls. They can also prove very destructive to exposed woodwork. Their coloration is variable, with some individuals being much paler than others. A few even border on white, but their crest coloration always serves to distinguish them easily from the closely-related white Umbrella Cockatoo *(C. alba)*, which is also slightly smaller.

As is usual with the *Cacatua* species, both parents share the task of incubating the two eggs for about 28 days. When the chicks hatch, it is quite common for the younger one to fall behind its nest-mate in terms of growth.

If this happens, you should remove it for hand-raising, or give it supplementary feeds. Otherwise, the chick is almost certain to die.

Left on their own, most pairs of these cockatoos will only rear one of their offspring successfully. Young birds will leave the nest when nearly 4 months old. The iris coloration of young cocks begins to darken from this point onward, although it is likely to be several years before they are mature enough to breed successfully.

### Goffin's Cockatoo— *Cacatua goffini*

Timor Laut (formerly Tanimbar Islands), Indonesia.

Mainly white, with salmon-pink suffusion on the lores and head feathers. Relatively small, vertical crest. Hens have more reddish irises than cocks, but this distinction is only apparent in good light. Young birds lack the pink suffusion on the heads of adults.

These cockatoos suddenly became available in large numbers during the early 1970s, as a result of forest clearance on the islands where they naturally occur. They have since proved highly destructive aviary occupants, and have bred successfully on numerous occasions, although they are not yet well-established in aviculture.

Two, sometimes three eggs form the usual clutch, and are incubated by both adults. Cocks sit during the day, with hens

Among Moluccan, or Salmon-crested, Cockatoos (*Cacatua moluccensis*), there is considerable variation in the degree of pinkish color attained by individuals. The most pronounced color is found in the crest and is most evident when the crest is erected.

taking over in the evening. The incubation period lasts 28 days, and the young fledge about ten weeks later. Like other cockatoos, adult birds tend to be nervous, but are quite hardy when acclimatized. Their lifespan is likely to extend over at least 50 years.

Umbrella Cockatoo, *Cacatua alba.*

# *Bibliography*

T. F. H. Publications offers the most comprehensive selection of books dealing with parrots in general, familiar groups, and the most popular and widely bred species. A selection of significant titles is presented below; these and many other works are available from your local pet shop, booksellers, or T.F.H. Publications itself.

*African Grey Parrots* by E. J. Mulawka (128pp, PS-870)

*The Atlas of Parrots of the World* by David Alderton (544pp, H-1109)

*Blue-Fronted Amazon Parrots* by E. J. Mulawka (128pp, PS-782)

*Breeding Conures* by Robbie Harris (122pp, H-1052)

*Budgerigar Handbook* by Ernest H. Hart (251pp, H-901)

*Cockatiel Handbook* by G. R. Allen & C. Allen (256pp, PS-741)

*Cockatiels! Pets—Breeding—Showing* by Nancy Reed (256pp, TS-140)

*Encyclopedia of Amazon Parrots* by Klaus Bosch & Ursula Wedde (128pp, H-1055)

*Encyclopedia of Budgerigars* by Georg Radtke (320pp, H-1027)

*Encyclopedia of Cockatiels* by G. A. Smith (256pp, PS-743)

*Encyclopedia of Parakeets* by K. Kolar & K. H. Spitzer (224pp, H-1094)

*The Grey Parrot* by Wolfgang De Grahl (224pp, H-1088)

*Grey-cheeked Parakeets* by Robbie Harris (160pp, PS-830)

*Handbook of Amazon Parrots* by A. E. Decoteau (256pp, H-1025)

*Handbook of Cockatoos* by A. E. Decoteau (160pp, H-1030)

*Handbook of Lovebirds* by Horst Bielfeld (117pp, H-1040)

*Handbook of Macaws* by A. E. Decoteau (128pp, H-1044)

*Keeping and Breeding Parrots* by Carl Aschenborn (160pp, TS-110)

and Lorikeets by Rosemary Low (180pp, PS-773)

*Parrakeets of the World* by Matthew M. Vriends (352pp, H-101)

*Parrots and Related Birds* by H. J. Bates & R. L. Busenbark (494 pp, H-912)

*Parrots of the World* by J. M. Forshaw (584pp, PS-753)

*The Professional's Book of Budgerigars* by Maja Müller-Bierl (144pp, TS-138)

*The Professional's Book of Conures* by John Coborn (144pp, TS-159)

*Taming and Training Parrots* by E. J. Mulawka (349pp, H-1019)

*Training Your Parrot* by Kevin P. Murphy (192pp, H-1056)

*The World of Cockatoos* by Karl Diefenbach (208pp, H-1072)

*The World of Lovebirds* by J. Brockmann & W. Lantermann (192pp, H-1092)

*The World of Macaws* by Dieter Hoppe (168pp, H-1079)

*Yellow-Fronted Amazon Parrots* by E. J. Mulawka (128pp, PS-781)

# *Index*

A group of lovebirds,
including the Madagascar,
the Abyssinian, Fischer's,
Masked, and Peach-faced.